Eat Well For Less

Eat Well For Less

BBC
BOOKS

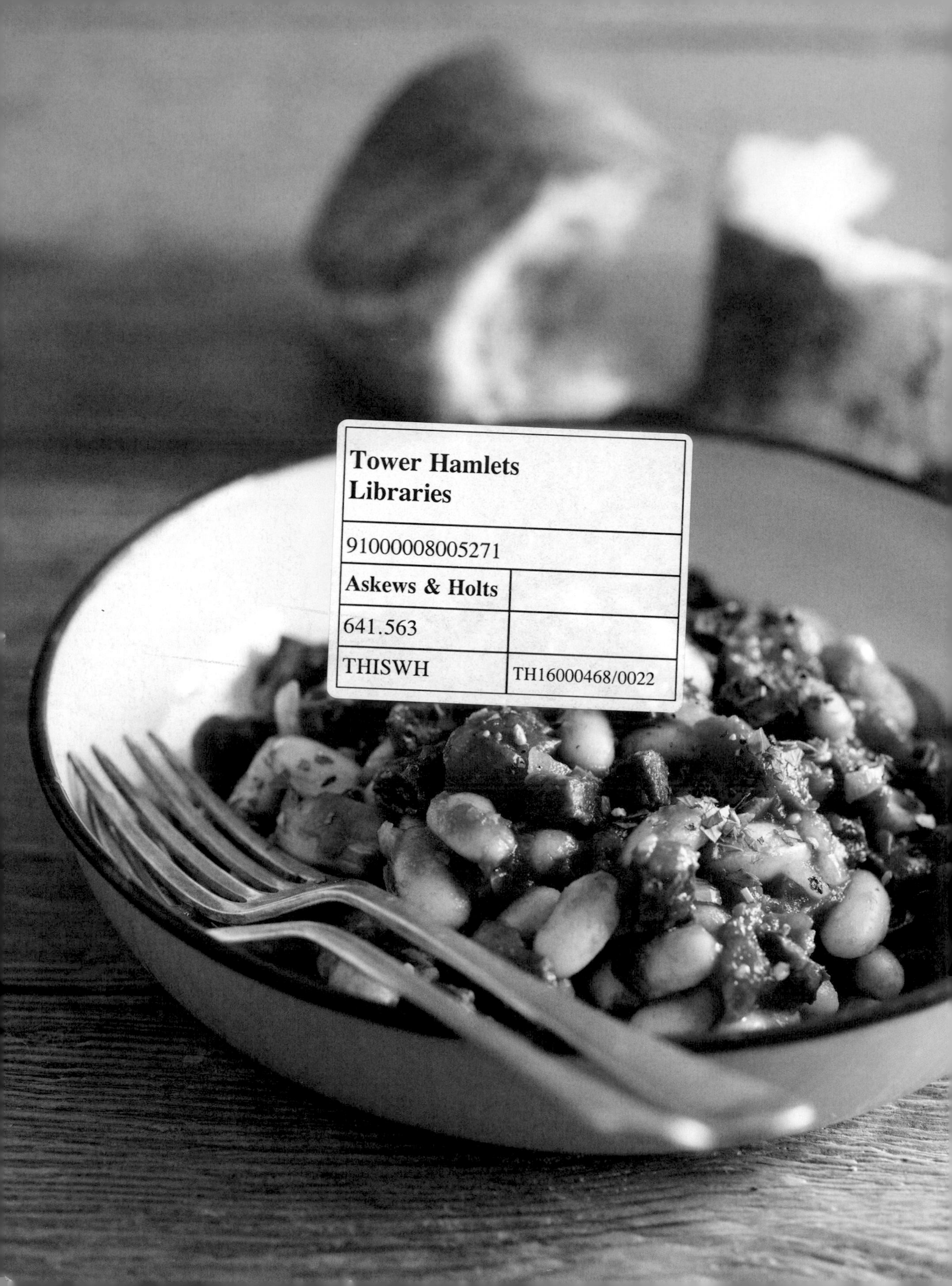

Contents

7   **Foreword by Gregg Wallace and Chris Bavin**

8   Tips and techniques

10   What kind of shopper are you?

14   Useful store cupboard ingredients

22   Equipment

24   Set your budget – and stick to it!

26   Healthy family food

32   Family Favourites

80   Quick and Simple Suppers

110   Celebrations and Feasts

146   Love your Leftovers

162   Treats and Snacks

192   Storing food

196   Timesaving tips

198   Meal planning

206   Food waste

210   Conversion charts

212   Index

221   Acknowledgements

Foreword by Gregg Wallace and Chris Bavin

They say you shouldn't judge a book by its cover, well this might be the exception, because this book will do exactly what it says on the cover! We want to show you how you can save money on your food bill without compromising on quality or enjoyment – and this book is full of tasty, simple recipes that will do just that. As we travel around the country making the series, we realise that none of the issues are unique. We all waste food, don't always make lists, are reluctant to try cheaper alternatives and spend far too much money on things we don't need to. We want to help you to change, and hope this book will inspire you to start making those simple changes that, in the long run, will mean the savings really add up.

If you received your food bill once a year, you'd be horrified and would do everything in your power to reduce it. But as we're making lots of small purchases, the total value doesn't really register. So one of the most important things you can do is shop around – not just by visiting high street grocers, fishmongers and butchers – who are a great source of information as well as often great value for money - but also shop around within the supermarket. Don't automatically pick up your usual brand week after week, try different ones. And if you don't like it, try a different one the week later. Open your eyes and challenge your tastebuds! Be aware that sometimes you really are just paying for fancy packaging - or convenience – and that it doesn't necessarily mean that it's better, healthier or tastier…just more expensive!

One easy thing you need to do when looking to reduce your bill, is PLAN. Follow these simple rules on the right and you're well on your way to eating well for less.

Cooking from scratch can be daunting, either because you feel you don't have the confidence or the time. We hope this book will show you that cooking simple meals can be quick and easy and something you might even enjoy doing together as a family. And as an added bonus you'll be saving money too!

Gregg and Chris

How to Eat Well for Less?

✔ Sit down with the family and plan what you want to eat for the following week. It's really important that you do this together, as that way you'll all be happy!

✔ Once you've got your meal plan, write a shopping list of what you'll need to make those meals.

✔ With your list in hand, go to your cupboards, fridge and freezer and cross off whatever ingredients you already have.

✔ Now you'll have a list with only the things you need to buy. Stick to it! You'll not only save money, you'll also reduce your waste.

Tips and techniques

If you're new to cooking and feeling a bit nervous, here are a few tips to get you started.

✔ Read the recipe before you start and get everything you need in front of you. There's nothing worse than having your hands covered in food and trying to dig out a teaspoon. If you are missing an ingredient, see if it's something you can easily substitute with something you do have.

✔ Remember to defrost any frozen ingredients in good time – particularly meat, chicken or fish. Vegetables will defrost quickly during cooking. Remove any butter, eggs, etc. from the fridge to soften or warm up to room temperature if the recipe recommends it.

✔ If the recipe tells you to preheat the oven at the beginning, turn it on now. Grease and line any tins at the start, too.

✔ Wash your hands, put on a pinny, tie back long hair and make sure your work surface and equipment are clean. It's basic hygiene but it's so important with food preparation.

Get stuck in!

✔ Follow the recipe carefully – particularly if you are baking.

✔ Check the instructions on the packaging. For example, if it asks you to rinse rice before cooking, put it in a sieve and set it under cold running water. For rice, pasta, noodles, etc., check the cooking time – it can vary.

✔ Wash knives, other utensils and your chopping boards if they have been used for raw meat, poultry, fish, eggs or vegetables – or better still, have a few colour-coded boards for each ingredient to prevent any cross-contamination.

How do you know if it's cooked?

Undercooking in particular is a worry, but equally you don't want your hard work to go to waste by overcooking food.

- **Pasta**
  Cook until al dente – if you scoop out a piece of pasta it should be just firm to the bite, not chewy and definitely not soggy.
- **Chicken**
  When roasting a whole bird, pierce the thigh of the chicken with a sharp knife – slide the knife in, then out again. Any juices coming out should be clear and the tip of the knife should be very hot. If not, return to the oven for another 5 minutes and check again. For chicken breasts or drumsticks, cut into the thickest part of the meat and see if there is any pink meat; if there is, it needs cooking longer.
- **Meat**
  For roasts, arm yourself with a meat thermometer – the food should be 70°C in the middle when it is ready. Pork, burgers and sausages should all be cooked through until there is no pink meat, but it is ok to eat beef and lamb rare if you like it that way.
- **Fish**
  The flesh should flake away and be opaque all the way through.
- **Other foods**
  Any other foods should be hot in the middle when ready.

- ✔ Keep raw and cooked foods separate during preparation to prevent the spread of bacteria.
- ✘ Don't wash raw meat, chicken or fish, but do wash fruit and vegetables.

Clearing up

- ✔ Clear up as much as you can as you go along and then you won't be faced with a mess when you've finished eating.
- ✔ If there are any leftovers, cool them as quickly as possible at room temperature (ideally within 1 to 2 hours), then store in the fridge or freeze for another day. Remember, when you reheat the food make sure it is steaming hot all the way through, and don't reheat it more than once. Particular instructions are relevant to reheating rice – see page 208.
- ✔ If you are storing food, use plastic freezerproof containers. Don't use aluminium to store food as it is highly acidic and will affect the flavour of the foods. If you have only used half a tin of an ingredient, tip out the remainder into another container to store.

Glossary of cooking terms

Beat: Stir rapidly to make a mixture smooth using a whisk, spoon or mixer.

Blanch: Cook vegetables or fruit briefly in boiling water to seal in flavour and colour – to prepare for freezing or to make removing skin easier.

Blend: To thoroughly combine 2 or more ingredients, either by hand with a whisk or spoon, or with a mixer.

Boil: Heat a liquid until it is rapidly bubbling.

Caramelize: To heat sugar until it liquefies and becomes a golden brown syrup.

Cream: To beat ingredients, usually sugar and butter or margarine, until smooth, blended and fluffy.

Fold in: To spoon lighter ingredients, such as egg whites or flour, into heavier ones. The heavier ingredients are gently lifted over the lighter ones to encase them and keep as much air in as possible.

Marinate: To coat meat, fish or poultry in a sauce or paste so that the food takes on its flavours.

Parboil: To partially cook an ingredient by boiling – this is usually done before roasting to reduce the cooking time of that ingredient in the final dish.

Purée: To mash or blend food until completely smooth, usually in a food processor, blender or sieve.

Reduce: To thicken a liquid and concentrate its flavour by boiling it.

Roast: To cook a large piece of meat or poultry in an oven.

Rub in: To break down butter into smaller pieces so that it resembles breadcrumbs. Lift your hands up out of the mixture as you are do this, so that you are not just squishing the ingredients together.

Sauté or pan-fry: To cook food in a little oil or fat in a frying pan over a relatively high heat.

Simmer: To cook a liquid just below the boiling point; there will be lots of little bubbles.

Steam: To cook food on a rack or in a steamer set over boiling or simmering water in a covered pan.

Stew: To cook food in a sauce or liquid in a covered pan over a low heat.

Stir-fry: To cook chopped ingredients quickly over a high heat whilst constantly stirring.

Whisk: To beat ingredients (such as cream, eggs or salad dressings) with a fork or whisk to mix, blend or incorporate air.

What kind of shopper are you?

Do you know what you want before you head to the shops? Or are you buying on impulse? Are you shopping when you're easily persuadable? If you want to Eat Well for Less, the first steps are looking at how you shop, how much you spend each time you visit the shops, and how you can get into new, healthier habits.

So, what kind of shopper are you?

1 Bargain hunter

Oooh you love a bargain! Those offers at the end of aisles, 3 for 2s, buy one get one free, buy one get one half price, they just jump out at you above all the noise and colour in the store. You can't help yourself. Sadly, a lot of these end up in the bin, as you can't fit them into your weekly meals. But that won't stop you next time, those deals are just too good to resist…

2 Throwaway shopper

You don't think too much about your shopping trips, you just buy it and think about it later. It's a bit of a supermarket sweep; take the nearest item, don't check the dates or the prices and you don't think about whether it will last the week. Often the best-before date creeps up quicker than you think and you won't eat it then. Into the bin it goes and back to the supermarket you go…

The Stantons

3 Impulse buyer

Even with the best-laid plans you can't resist sticking something extra into the trolley. You can always convince yourself that you need that item, or perhaps just that you deserve it. It might get eaten, or it might take the place of a healthier option. Funny how fruit and veg doesn't have quite the same allure as those cakes or biscuits?

From Series One, the Stanton family threw away lots of food, and had a fear of the freezer!

4 Convenience shopper

Time is precious, you'd rather spend more on ready meals for the sheer convenience of not having to prepare it when you get home. Or you nip out for sandwiches because you just didn't get time to think last night what you'd have for lunch at work. Life's too short to spend hours in the kitchen, isn't it?

5 Stuck in a rut shopper

Shopping is a chore – you've lost the love for food. You buy the same things each week and prepare the same foods. It works for you because it's easy, but it's dull. You'd like to change things up a bit but you don't know how. That sweet potato looks really tempting and unusual, but you don't know what to do with it, so the Maris Pipers it is. Maybe next week?

Did you recognize yourself? The behaviours of each type of shopper have a significant impact on how you shop and how much you spend! A few small changes could make a big difference to your bank balance.

Remember that supermarkets are businesses first and foremost and they invest millions in working out how to get you to spend more in their stores. Walking into a supermarket you will be greeted with rows and rows of aisles packed with carefully selected products strategically placed for maximum appeal. Fruit and veg are often placed near the front of the shop – their freshness and rainbow of colours will entice you in, then once you've packed a few in your trolley, those cream cakes placed further back don't feel such a naughty purchase. You've got your five-a-day, why not have a treat too?!

Of course, sometimes you've just popped in for a pint of milk and you'll find yourself coming out loaded with shopping bags. That's because in tracking down the milk tucked somewhere at the back of the shop you'll have passed hundreds of other products that suddenly you think you need!

Even if you can pass along the aisles with blinkers on, the end-of-aisle promotions will often entice you over – people are 30% more likely to buy items at the end of the aisle than in the middle, because of their high visibility. So when you've navigated the shop and finally reach the till, you think you are safe. Not so. Here, just as you are almost home free, you are often treated to an array of magazines, easily pick-upable sweets and snacks that just scream 'pop me in your bag!' If you have children with you, often your fate is sealed.

But don't despair, you can resist temptation and reduce those bills (and bulging shopping bags) with a few simple changes.

Stick to the plan

Most overspending in supermarkets is down to poor planning and impulse buying. How often do you go in with a list? Do you stick to it, or do you come out with several items that were not on the list? Write yourself a list and stick to it! Even better, plan your meals for the week so you know exactly what you are going to cook and what you need – this will massively cut down on your wastage. This really is the golden rule – what's on your list is what you need, what gets added may get wasted. If you can, have a budget in mind, too and take only that amount of cash with you – no cards. You can then only spend as much as you have!

Basketcase

If you're just popping into the supermarket for a few items, pick up a basket. Psychologically this will help you buy less and, also importantly, to buy only as much as you can carry home. Grab a large trolley and you'll feel tempted to fill it. Ditto for travelling to the supermarket; if you only need a few things, walk down there and don't take the car. If you have to lug everything home you won't buy those heavy, overlarge items or unnecessary extras.

Get in the mood

How often do you pop into the supermarket on your way home from work after a long, tiring day? Or perhaps with small bouncing children after a sleepless night or ridiculously early start, nerves in tatters? Perhaps you haven't eaten all day and you're shopping to restock the empty fridge. All these scenarios will change how you feel about food. Shopping when you are tired and hungry is a big no-no – you will be drawn to expensive and unhealthy ready meals or part-prepared foods as they seem the quick, easy option to get you back on track. Or you might stock up on comfort foods, biscuits, cakes and other foods that offer that instant sugar kick and hug on a bad day.

Too good to be true?

Those offers can look amazing, but if you look really closely are they as good as you think? Read the small print carefully. Is it really cheaper to buy 3 rather than 2, or buy one get one free; is £3 for 2 items individually priced at £1.50 a bargain? Are the weights of multibuy offers the same across the board? Sometimes some products show a weight in kilos and others in grams, when you compare the two is it such a good deal? And remember, these deals can only be bargains if you're actually going to use the goods!

Stay out of the shops

Online shopping is a brilliant modern convenience that allows you to get your shopping done without having to leave the house. Perfect if you can't make time to get there or don't want to shop when you're not in the optimum mood (see above), but it also allows you to stick to a budget and not get distracted by offers and unnecessary items or be pressured into buying unhealthy snacks by persistent children! You have ultimate control of what's in your basket.

Top tips for shopper types

1 Bargain hunter

✔ Work out if products are good value by comparing prices per 100g.
✔ Walk past promotions, think about them and go back if you really think they are worth it.
✔ Use your bargains. Keep an eye on the dates and cook and freeze them if the use-by date is imminent.

2 Throwaway shopper

✘ Don't take the oldest stock with the soonest use-by date, reach to the back of the shelf to get the freshest items.
✔ 'Best before' is about quality and food at that can still be safe to eat, but 'use by' is about safety and after that date food shouldn't be eaten.
✔ Store food properly so that it lasts for as long as possible.
✔ Love your leftovers - use them in other recipes to save waste.

3 Impulse buyer

✔ Before you shop, plan your meals and make a list of what you need.
✔ Limit your trips to the supermarket to reduce the temptation to impulse buy there.
✔ Pay attention to your shopping habits. Think before you pick up.

4 Convenience shopper

✔ Add up how much you spend on takeaway sandwiches, snacks and drinks. It could be enough to make you rethink your habits!
✔ Find some quick, easy recipes that you can cook in minutes when you get home instead of buying ready meals.
✔ Look through our recipes for home-cooked versions of your favourite convenience dishes.

5 Stuck in a rut shopper

✔ Get online or into those cookery books and aim to try a new food or ingredient every week.
✔ Add a twist to your favourite meals look up new recipes or just add another ingredient.

Useful store cupboard ingredients

Having a kitchen well-stocked with a good range of ingredients makes cooking easier on busy weeknights meaning you can better resist the temptation to pick up a ready meal on the way home or phone for a pizza. Save your pennies and plunder your cupboards for something healthy, homemade and inexpensive.

Store-cupboard staples

Often tinned or dried, these are your ingredients that tend to have a long shelf life. This lists looks like a lot, but they do last and often a little goes a long way. Whenever you restock your shelves, think like a supermarket and put the newer tins or packets at the back, behind the older ones, so that you don't waste food by not noticing it reaching its sell-by date.

The Warners

The Warner family loved brands, and had a lot of bad habits to break!

Rice, pasta, grains and pulses

- **Rice**
  Makes a good base for risottos, paellas or pilafs, or as an accompaniment to stews, curries and stir-fries. Use wholegrain ideally, or have white and perhaps basmati and risotto rice, too.
- **Dried pasta**
  Any size, any shape. Perfect for pasta bakes or with homemade sauces. You can even use leftovers in salads, soups and stews.
- **Dried noodles (egg or rice)**
  Great for stir-fries, soups and curries.
- **Couscous, bulgur, pearl barley, farro, quinoa**
  All packed with protein. Excellent in tagines or stews or as the base for a salad and brilliant for bulking out stews and soups.
- **Pulses and beans**
  Buy dried or tinned (much less faff) chickpeas, cannellini, kidney and butter beans and lentils. Don't forget the humble baked beans, either, which work well on their own or added to stews. Packed with protein they make an excellent alternative to more expensive meat.

Tins

- **Vegetables**
  Whole plum tomatoes – essential for sauces, soups, stews and casseroles – the ultimate all-rounder.

- **Fish**

  Tuna, salmon, sardines or anchovies can be transformed into fishcakes or add flavour to simple pasta sauces or salads.
- **Light coconut milk**

  A popular ingredient at the moment, but particularly good for soups and curries to add a creamy flavour without the calories!
- **Fruit**

  Tins of peaches, pineapple, cherries, mandarin, etc. are perfect when the fresh versions are out of season. Add to yoghurt, top with granola for a speedy crumble, cover with pastry for a simple pie or just eat as a snack. Try to buy fruit in its juice rather than in syrup, to reduce the sugar content.

Herbs and spices

Great for adding all-important flavour. This is a long list to cover all tastes, but play around with recipes and see which of these you prefer. You don't need to buy them all at once, you can build up your collection bit by bit.

Oregano, **smoked paprika**, **chilli** (flakes or powder, mild or hot), **cinnamon**, **cumin**, **coriander**, **curry powder** or paste, **five-spice**, **turmeric**, **ginger**, **fennel seeds**.

You can even freeze some fresh herbs to extend their season; a few leaves into ice-cube trays with enough water to cover then drop the frozen cubes into sauces and stews as needed. Fresh chillies also freeze well, as do curry and bay leaves.

Seasonings

- **Sea salt**

  Sea salt flakes are good and natural.
- **Black peppercorns**

  They stay fresher if ground on demand.
- **Soy sauce**

  Good for Asian dishes, marinades and sauces.

- **Good-quality stock cubes**

  Try the low-salt versions.
- **Tomato purée**

  Adds a concentrated tomato flavour.

Jars & bottles

- **Honey**

  Add a touch of sweetness to sauces and marinades.
- **Condiments**

  Keep a stash of your favourites: ketchup, mayonnaise, brown sauce, mustard.

Oils and vinegars

Use vegetable, rapeseed or groundnut oil for cooking and keep the more expensive olive oil for dressings and drizzling over dishes. Red wine, white wine, cider and balsamic vinegars are all useful for marinades, dressings and sauces.

Baking staples and extras

- **Plain flour**

  For thickening sauces, coating meat, fish and veggies for frying, and baking.
- **Self-raising flour and baking powder**

  For cakes and bakes.
- **Bread flour and dried yeast**

  For making bread and pizza dough.
- **Cocoa powder and vanilla extract**

  For flavouring.
- **Caster, granulated and icing sugars**
- **Porridge oats**

  Useful for baking cookies, flapjacks and crumbles but also perfect for a filling breakfast in their own right.
- **Nuts and seeds**

  Keep a stock of your favourites for toasting and sprinkling over salads, soups and stews, or onto yoghurt, or just to nibble on as a healthy snack.

Fridge

- **Dairy**
  When buying cheese, the stronger the flavour, the less you need to use, which is good for the wallet and your waistline; choose mature over mild Cheddar. Look for cheaper cheeses too, swap out Parmesan for the cheaper Grana Padano, use basic mozzarella in cooking. A supply of plain yoghurt is useful for marinades, sauces or with frozen or tinned fruit or cereal. Milk and butter are staples, as is bread.
- **Vegetables and salad**
  Keep a supply of your favourite ingredients from whatever is in season.
- **Eggs**
  Brilliant for a speedy breakfast, supper and, of course, for baking.

The Scotts

The Scott family loved freezer food, and had a big problem with waste!

Love your freezer

Aside from your cupboards and the fridge, the key to having a good source of ingredients to hand is to make friends with your freezer. This is when you can really make the most of those multibuy bargains or mark-downs, and it is the perfect place to keep leftovers or pre-prepared food in portions for another day. Always freeze on the day of purchase or preparing, and make sure the items are dated. Most items can be stored in the freezer for a month or two.

- **Bread**
  Freeze packs of bread rolls, muffins, pittas, tortillas, homemade pizza bases and sliced bread. Defrost before eating/cooking or toast straight from the freezer.
- **Meat, poultry and fish**
  Frozen or fresh that's on offer. Fish fillets make great meals on standby, as do all sorts of cuts of meat or poultry. Also good for prawns or mixed seafood. You will often find it can be cheaper to buy sides of salmon, etc., and cut them up yourself into portions rather than buying pre-portioned food.
- **Fruit and vegetables**
  Much cheaper than fresh and because they are frozen at source or within a couple of hours of being picked, they're often fresher, too, and retain more nutrients. Keep a stock of peas, broad beans, spinach, cauliflower, green beans, broccoli, sweetcorn, and perhaps some out of season fruits such as berries, mango chunks or cherries.
- **Batch cooking**
  If you've succumbed to that meat multi-buy offer and the sell-by date is approaching, or you have an hour or two free to get ahead for the week, batch-cook stews, casseroles, Bolognese sauces, etc. and freeze them in portions. An instant meal on a busy day.

Choosing ingredients

How you choose your ingredients is obviously a major factor in how much you spend on your weekly shop. You may have got stuck in bad shopping habits that are just that, a habit, so it's time to break the cycle and change the way you shop. Look back to 'What kind of shopper are you?' and the tips that are relevant to you and bear these in mind when you go out to buy food.

There are, of course, a few general pointers that we can all remember to help us keep the costs down.

Step outside your comfort zone

No, not as in buying weird and exotic ingredients (although that's a great idea as long as you know what to do with them!) but simply try shopping in new places. Online shopping or doing your weekly shop in the same supermarket is convenient but are you getting the best deals there? Take a calculator and even a pad of paper and make notes of prices so you can compare them; it might take a bit of research to get this sort of information, but it will be worth it in the end if it saves you money.

Local markets

Try these for fruit and veg, meat, poultry, fish and even cheeses. You might be surprised at how much cheaper these can be. The products may not always be beautifully shaped or packaged but chances are they will taste as good!

Cash and carry

Try these for bulk buys of tinned and dried produce – essentially longlife foodstuffs. You can do this once a month, and if you don't have enough storage space why not split your purchases with friends or family?

Shop local

Although the smaller shops can be harder to find on the high street in cities, they are still there. Make friends with your butcher, fishmonger, greengrocer they are an invaluable source of advice on the best cuts you can use to help you to feed your family on a budget.

Try another supermarket

Don't be a snob about where you buy your food. Discount supermarkets can offer really good value on branded or own-brand goods that are often just as good as those from more expensive supermarkets.

Think about what you are buying

When you plan your meals, think about what you are using. Can you substitute some ingredients for cheaper ones, or bulk out meat dishes by replacing a proportion of the meat with less expensive ingredients, such as veg, pulses or beans?

Consider the cut

Try different cuts of meat or poultry. The prime cuts of beef, for example, are sirloin, fillet and rib-eye, but flat-iron makes a good cheaper alternative. Or you could try brisket or shin of beef. With chicken, breast fillets are the expensive cuts but thighs or legs are much cheaper and are delicious roasted or slow-cooked in sauces. Slow-cooking gives you great flavours at a much lower cost, particularly if the meat is on the bone – the gentle, lengthy cooking gradually breaks down the fibres in the meats until they are melt-in-the-mouth delicious.

Stay in season

Use fruits and veg that are in season; that means not buying fresh strawberries in winter when they are at their most expensive. Their prices are higher because they will have been grown in warmer climes and flown into the UK or grown under heat, which has its own costs to the producer.

Perfect specimens

Do you really need perfectly straight carrots or beautifully round potatoes if you are just going to chop, slice or mash them? Such aesthetically pleasing fruit and veg come at a price to the consumer and the producer. It's fine to eat crooked carrots, knobbly fruit and wonky potatoes!

Frozen foods

Often cheaper than fresh and for many ingredients they can be fresher as they are frozen so quickly after preparation – by the time fresh produce hits the shelves it can often have lost roughly half its original amount of nutrients. Frozen fish can be as much as 50% cheaper than fresh. Keeping a stock of frozen foods in the freezer also means you have dinner on demand and also are less likely to waste it as it can be stored so much longer than fresh and you only take out what you need when you need it.

Convenience food

These might be convenient but you are paying for the privilege. Pre-cut and pre-prepped fruit, veggies and salad can cost twice as much as the whole ingredients and can lose their nutrients rapidly and deteriorate quicker than the unprepared product. As for ready meals, these are a very expensive way of eating – and can be unhealthy! Yes, they can be cooked in minutes, but so can a stir-fry. Ditch those microwave dinners and get to know your kitchen again.

Think ahead

Planning is such an important factor in saving money on your food shops. If you've worked out what you will be cooking and what you need (rather than quite fancy…) and are sticking to the list, that's the first step to saving pennies, but bear in mind a few other factors to get the most from your basket…

Check the dates

When choosing fresh foods, check the use-by dates on the packaging and try to pick those that have the longest life. Unless you're going to freeze it or use it on the day of purchase, buying too far in advance may mean it ends up lurking at the back of the fridge until it passes its date and ends up in the bin.

Do you really need it?

Don't overbuy. Don't get swayed by those tempting multibuy offers if you know you won't really get through three bags of bananas before they go off. Think about eating smaller portions, too. Do you need that much food? Would it be healthier to buy less and eat less?

Where will it go?

Do you have enough cupboard/freezer/fridge space for everything you are buying? If ingredients are not stored correctly they will degrade faster. Have you checked your cupboards before you left? Don't buy another jar of jam if there are already four more at the back of the cupboard. Stop and think before you buy luxury items, too. Are you just being tempted by the beautiful packaging? Won't the own label version be just as good as the premium brand? Try it, it might surprise you.

The Booths

The Booth family's biggest problem was overbuying and impulse shopping!

Equipment

You don't need loads of expensive kit and gadgets to be able to cook healthy, inexpensive meals from scratch. Keep those for the Christmas list and stock up on the essentials first. As much as anything, you want to keep your worktops clear for prepping food – that's not easy if it's covered in machines!

Essentials

- **Saucepans**
  A couple in different sizes with lids. Preferably non-stick.
- **Frying pan**
  Again, non-stick and preferably with a lid. If you're a fan of pancakes or omelettes it's worth getting a smaller, thin-edged frying pan for these.
- **Wok**
  OK, not essential, but really, really useful if you're a fan of stir-frying. Probably the quickest meal you can make and one that you can pack with veggies! Get a decent-quality one and it will last for ages. If you've got a Chinese supermarket nearby you could pick one up pretty cheaply.
- **Colander and sieve**
  Plastic or metal, great for draining foods and sifting dry ingredients.
- **Mixing bowl**
  At least one large one and perhaps a smaller one, too, if you get the baking bug. Ideally get a heatproof one (possibly even microwave-safe too) if you are going to be using it to melt chocolate, etc.
- **Chopping board and a couple of sharp kitchen knives**
  One for chopping or carving, another for cutting fruit and veg. Wooden chopping boards are durable and attractive, plastic are also great and very hygienic. If you can stretch to it, get a few boards in different colours and keep them separate for prepping meat, fish and veg.
- **Kitchen scissors**
- **Vegetable peeler**
  Makes peeling all that veg a speedier job!
- **Can opener**
- **Grater**
  A simple box grater can cover a lot of your cooking situations.

The Scotts

Mum Kate hardly ever cooked from scratch, but learned how to make a family favourite – chips!

- **Whisk**
  Essential for whipping cream and egg whites.
- **Wooden spoon**
  Good for baking and for stirring foods in non-stick saucepans.
- **Spatula and fish slices**
  Silicone ones best for non-stick surfaces.
- **Potato masher**
  Not just for potatoes, great for parsnip, butternut squash, carrots, etc.
- **Hand-held blender**
  If you're short of kitchen space, a hand-held blender makes a great alternative to an electric worktop blender. Essential for perfectly blended soups, sauces and smoothies.
- **Measuring jug**
  Preferably heatproof for measuring out hot water/stock.
- **Scales**
  Particularly important for portion control to weigh out ingredients but also essential for successful baking.
- **Roasting tin**
- **Baking sheet**
- **12-hole cupcake tray and a couple of cake tins**
- **Baking parchment, cling film, tin foil and kitchen roll**
- **Baking dish**
  For pasta bakes, lasagne, shepherd's pie, etc.
- **Pepper and salt mills**
  Much cheaper to grind your own than buy ready ground salt and pepper, and you'll get a better flavour from them.
- **Oven glove and tea towels**
- **Freezerproof and microwaveable containers**
  Ideal for storing those leftovers or foods that you batch-cook for another day.
- **Wire rack**
  For cooling any baked goods or use your grill rack!

Gadgets and kit for the wish list

- **Garlic press**
  Good for speed and precision, makes life a lot easier, probably should be an essential!
- **Microplane zester**
  Makes zesting and fine grating a dream.
- **Spiralizer**
  A speedy way to get your 5 a day.
- **Food processor**
  Speeds up blending, cake making, making breadcrumbs, pastry making and numerous other laborious jobs!
- **Palette knife, pastry brush, rolling pin**
  The list goes on when it comes to kit for baking, depending on whether you get the bug!

- **Slow cooker**
  Fashionable once again, you can throw together a recipe in the morning and leave it to cook all day ready for when you get home. Also the perfect way to cook those cheaper cuts of meat. They come in all different sizes depending on the size of your family or kitchen and are pretty inexpensive. If you can, get one with a timer. Another good time-saver is a pressure cooker.

Set your budget – and stick to it!

How much money you have to spend on food depends on your individual circumstances, expenditure on other household items – such as rent/mortgage and other bills – as well as how many people are in your family. Roughly speaking, you should allocate between 10 and 15 per cent of your net income to food and grocery shopping. According to the Office for National Statistics, the average household spends £81.40 on food and drink each week, but with a little forward planning and some careful shopping you could significantly reduce that figure for a family of four.

If budgeting isn't your strong point, there are lots of budget calculators available online that can help you get to grips with your finances and help you decide how much you can afford to spend on food.

With the cost of living outstripping wages, more families than ever are feeling the pinch and having to really look hard at their spending. Food is an essential expenditure, not a luxury, so how can you eat well for less so that you can keep on top of your bills and maybe even have some spare cash to splash out on other things? Here are the key things you need to think about, which will all be explored in more detail throughout the book.

MOT your spending habits

Look at your spending and try to identify where you are going wrong (see page 10). Often just seeing the figures in front of you is enough to make you realize you need to rethink the way you shop. Eating well for less is about changing bad habits for new, healthier ones – your body and wallet will benefit! Setting a budget doesn't have to mean the end to all luxuries, but do you really need them every day?

Get cooking!

Ditch the expensive ready meals and pre-prepared ingredients and get back to basics. Cooking from scratch is not just a cheaper way to eat, but healthier too. Take breakfast and even lunch to work and stop buying expensive coffees on the way – a working couple could each spend £71.10 a week on takeaway lunches, coffee and snacks, which works out at an eyewatering £4000 a year between them both!

Planning

Plan your weekly meals (see page 198), write a shopping list only for what you need to buy, and try to make that shop the only one, rather than nipping out for food here and there across the week. Don't get sidetracked by tempting offers or treats when you're going round the shops – stick to the list and you'll stick to your budget.

Keep it fresh

Storing your food properly means you can keep it in optimum condition for longer, which means you won't be throwing away as much limp lettuce, dubious-smelling dairy or grey-looking meat, which is like throwing cash in the bin. See page 192 for advice on how to store food.

Make smart food swaps

Think about your ingredients when you're out shopping – compare prices, try own-brand products, swap out fresh for frozen or tinned. You'll be amazed at how much prices can vary, and not necessarily at the expense of quality (see page 18).

Learn to love your leftovers

At the end of each meal, stop before you start clearing up and scraping those plates into the bin. Is there anything that can be served up again for lunch or dinner, or used to bulk out another meal? Think about what you have left and how you can reuse it – it's not just about saving money or reducing waste, but it can also cut your preparation time for another dinner!

Go meat-free

Meat is expensive, so why not try to ditch it a few days a week? Even the most hardened carnivore can be surprised at how delicious vegetarian recipes can be – not to mention an instant boost to getting your 5 a day! So don't relegate your veg to the sidelines, put vibrant, colourful vegetables centre stage and feel the benefits to your wallet and your health.

Grow your own

Don't waste money on expensive bags of herbs and salad that wilt and blacken in your fridge, grow your own for a fraction of the price. No matter how small your outdoor space, whether it's a garden, a patio, a balcony or just a windowsill, you could grow a few tasty additions to perk up your recipes. Sprinkle some seeds into a few pots and you can have a supply of herbs handy for snipping whenever you need them. Grow some speedy salad like rocket and you can have a salad at your fingertips and boost your veg intake, too. It's a great way to get the kids interested in eating healthily, and who knows, you might get the gardening bug and get growing more fruit and veg.

The Parsons

The Parsons were creatures of habit, and their food spend was out of control!

Healthy family food

Eating well for less is not just about saving money, but also about eating healthily. Fruit and vegetables play an important part in a healthy diet, and the advice from the World Health Organization is that there are significant health benefits to be had by eating at least five portions of 80g of fruit and veg each day, including a lowered risk of heart disease, stroke and some cancers.

Fill up on your five a day

There is a wide range of fruit and vegetables available all year round, all of which are a good source of vitamins and minerals to varying degrees, including folate, vitamin C and potassium. They are also an excellent source of dietary fibre, which helps maintain a healthy gut and prevents constipation. A diet high in fibre can also reduce the risk of bowel cancer. Most fruits and veg are low in fat and calories, too, which makes them a healthy snack choice – although be warned that dried fruits are higher in calories and sugar than fresh, so should be eaten in smaller quantities.

You can get your 5 a day in many forms – fresh, frozen, tinned, dried and juiced. There is a huge variety of fruit and veg to pick from so you can always find something you like, and in some form that will suit your budget. Remember, though, that potatoes do not count as part of your 5 a day, as they mostly contain starch.

What is a portion?

A single portion should weigh about 80g, which is roughly equivalent to:

- 1 apple, orange, banana or pear
- 1 large slice of melon or pineapple
- 2 plums, kiwi fruit or satsumas
- 3 tablespoons cooked vegetables
- A dessert bowl of salad
- 1 glass of pure fruit juice
  (this includes from concentrate)
  NB this only counts as one portion no matter how much you drink in a day.
- 1 tablespoon dried fruit
- 3 sticks of celery, 1 medium raw carrot OR 5cm piece of cucumber or 7 cherry tomatoes

For children, a portion is as much as they can hold in their hand.

Five a day on a budget

You can still fill your trolley with your 5 a day even if you are on a budget.

✔ Buy fruit and vegetables loose rather than pre-packaged – this can be significantly cheaper.

✔ Choose fruits and veg that are in season (see chart page 28) – they are cheaper when they are produced in abundance and locally without the expense of enhanced growing conditions or being flown in from other countries. Eating in season also means that you are eating the nutrients that your body needs at a particular time of year.

✔ Try local markets as well as supermarkets, as you might find them cheaper. Also look for marked-down ingredients in supermarkets and cook them up in stews, soups and casseroles or freeze them (see page 194).

✔ Swap out snacks such as crisps and chocolate bars with a piece of fruit, not only is it healthier, it is also cheaper – a piece of fruit can cost half as much as these sugary items.

✔ If you find that fresh ingredients are too expensive, stock up on frozen or tinned ones – they are often just as fresh, if not more so, and you can have them on standby without worrying about having to use them up quickly before their use-by date.

✔ Adding vegetables to stews, curries or casseroles is a really economical way to bulk out meaty dishes.

Seasonal calendar for locally-grown fruit and veg

	Spring (March-May)	Summer (June-Aug)	Autumn (Sept-Nov)	Winter (Dec-Feb)
Fruit	Rhubarb	Blueberries	Apples	Apples
		Currants	Blackberries	Pears
		Elderflowers	Damsons	
		Greengages	Elderberries	
		Loganberries	Pears	
		Plums	Plums	
		Raspberries	Quince	
		Strawberries	Sloes	
Vegetables	Asparagus	Aubergine	Beetroot	Beetroot
	Cauliflower	Beetroot	Carrot	Brussels Sprouts
	Cucumber	Broad Beans	Celeriac	Cabbage
	Jersey Royal New	Broccoli	Fennel	Cauliflower
	Potatoes	Carrots	Field Mushrooms	Celeriac
	Purple Sprouting	Courgettes	Kale	Chicory
	Broccoli	Cucumber	Leeks	Fennel
	Radishes	Fennel	Lettuce	Jerusalem
	Savoy Cabbage	Fresh Peas	Marrow	Artichoke
	Sorrel	Garlic	Potatoes	Kale
	Spinach	Green Beans	Pumpkin	Leeks
	Spring Greens	Lettuce and	Rocket	Parsnips
	Spring Onion	Salad Leaves	Sorrel	Potatoes
	Watercress	New potatoes	Squashes	Red Cabbage
		Radishes	Sweetcorn	Swede
		Rocket	Tomatoes	Turnips
		Runner Beans	Watercress	
		Spring Onions		
		Sorrel		
		Tomatoes		
		Watercress		

Five a day throughout the day

If you struggle to eat all your 5 a day each day, keep a copy of the eatwell plate on your fridge to remind yourself to buy fruit and veg in larger quantities than your usual meat, carbs, dairy foods and high-fat products. It is a good visual and colourful reminder!

Still stuck? Try a few of these ideas to sneak those essential fruits and veg into your daily diet…

Breakfast

✔ Add fresh, frozen or tinned berries or sliced apple or banana to pancakes, natural yoghurt or fromage frais, porridge or cereal. Blend them up into smoothies – a smoothie can contain up to 2 portions of your 5 a day if you choose carefully; mash bananas or fresh strawberries and whisk into milk for a delicious milkshake.

✔ Make your own granola or muesli and add your favourite dried fruits. If you like, you can serve it up with milk and some fresh fruit, too.

✔ Grill mushrooms or tomatoes and serve alongside scrambled eggs or even bacon for a treat.

Snacks

✔ Snack on dried fruits or fresh fruit – ½–1 tablespoon currants or raisins or 2 dried apricots or prunes equal 1 portion. Try an apple, pear, banana or a couple of satsumas. Or even go for veg snacks, try carrot, celery, pepper or cucumber sticks.

✔ Give your children fruit for snacks instead of sweets. Bananas, apples, satsumas, small bunches of grapes or small tins of fruit are ideal in lunchboxes. Try small packets of dried fruit, too.

Fruit and vegetables are one of the most important parts of your diet. Here's how the other food groups should fit in:

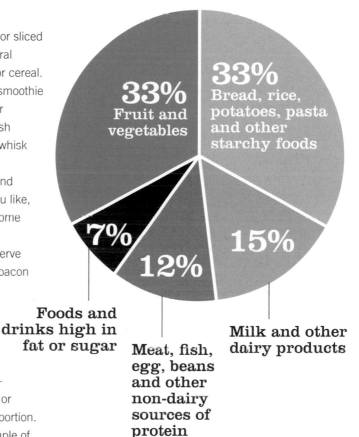

33% Fruit and vegetables

33% Bread, rice, potatoes, pasta and other starchy foods

15% Milk and other dairy products

12% Meat, fish, egg, beans and other non-dairy sources of protein

7% Foods and drinks high in fat or sugar

Lunch

✔ Make up a salad, pack a sandwich with lettuce, tomatoes, cucumber, peppers or grated carrot or prepare a colourful plate of crudités to eat with a low-fat dip or houmous. Wash it down with freshly squeezed unsweetened fruit juice.

✔ Whizz up some soup using whatever veg you have in the fridge or following a recipe. Add some beans and pulses, too, as they provide one portion of your 5 a day (although no matter how many beans, pulses and lentils you eat in a day it is still only one portion).

Dad Chris usually bought food on the way to work, but Gregg and Chris found a savvy swap to save money!

The Scotts

Dinner

✔ Make sure you have at least two portions of different veg on your plate – not potatoes. Try serving peas or green beans alongside a shepherd's pie or fish pie or a salad alongside meat or chicken. Substitute pasta with spiralized courgette and serve it with sauces made from tomatoes rather than cream or cheese.

✔ Add tinned or chopped vegetables such as carrots, peas or mushrooms to soups, stews, Bolognese sauce or homemade burgers.

✔ Cook up a stir-fry – this is the perfect opportunity to really bump up your vegetables intake.

✔ Eat the rainbow – pack in peppers, onion, broccoli, beansprouts, carrots. It's also a brilliant way to use up any stray vegetables in your fridge.

✔ Fruit salad makes a great pudding, and any leftovers can always be eaten for breakfast. Or stew up some fruit and make it into a crumble. If you've got a fruit fussy child, tempt them to eat fruit by adding tinned, fresh or (thawed) frozen fruit to jellies.

✔ In summer, pile fruit onto skewers and also make kebabs with meat, chicken and prawns, alternating with chunks of vegetables that you can pop on the barbecue. Sweetcorn on the cob and baked bananas in their skins are also great on a grill.

Eat the rainbow!

Your 5 a day should consist of as many different-coloured varieties as possible. If you need a little inspiration to pick your selection, here are the benefits of the different pigments of fruit and vegetables:

Red

Tomatoes, red peppers, radishes, rhubarb, strawberries, raspberries, cherries
Contain: *Lycopene* – An age-defying antioxidant, which may protect cells in the prevention of heart disease, skin from sun damage and against certain cancers.

Yellow

Grapefruits, bananas, pineapples, sweetcorn, squash, yellow peppers, yellow lentils, chickpeas
Contain: *Beta-cryptoxanthin* – A phyto-chemical that helps with vitamin and mineral exchange between cells. May also help to protect against rheumatoid arthritis and heart disease.

Purple

Raisins, currants, sultanas, prunes, figs, damsons, plums, blueberries, blackcurrants, blackberries, grapes, aubergine, beetroot, kidney beans
Contain: *Anthocyanidin* – This protects against pain and inflammation, may support healthy blood pressure and may also have anti-ageing properties by preventing the breakdown of collagen in the skin.

Orange

Oranges, nectarines, peaches, mango, salsumas, apricots, sweet potato, carrots, red lentils, baked beans
Contain: *Alpha* and *Beta-carotene* – This gets converted to vitamin A in the body, which is essential for vision, immune function and antioxidants that protect your skin from ultraviolet damage. It also builds new cells and is good for bone health.

Green

Avocado, melon, gooseberries, apples, pears, courgettes, cucumber, peas, spinach lettuce/salad leaves, broccoli, cabbage, asparagus, kale, spring greens
Contain: *Lutein* – A carotenoid that's good for skin hydration and elasticity, and helps reduce the risk of cataracts and protects the eyes. *Isothiocyanates* – This is an anticarcinogenic. Avocados and leafy greens are also rich in vitamin E, which can help prevent wrinkles and strengthens cell membranes.

Family Favourites

1

Shepherd's pie

SERVES 4–6

1 tbsp rapeseed oil
450g lean minced lamb
1 large red onion, finely
   chopped
1 garlic clove, finely chopped
3 carrots, peeled and finely
   chopped
100g split red lentils
1 tbsp tomato ketchup
400g tin chopped tomatoes
350ml lamb or beef stock
   (you can use a stock cube
   dissolved in boiling water)
3 tbsp chopped parsley, plus
   extra to garnish (optional)
sea salt and freshly ground
   black pepper, to taste

Potato topping
750g floury potatoes, peeled
   and cut into chunks
75ml semi-skimmed milk
25g butter

Tips
• If you let the meat go
   cold before topping, it's
   easier to spread the
   mash over.
• You can make the whole
   dish the day before,
   keep it in the fridge,
   covered, then bake it
   for 30 minutes when
   you want to eat it.

An old-school, comforting shepherd's pie, but the addition of red lentils adds an unusual twist. You could do the same with any mince dish to stretch your money a little further as lentils are cheaper than a meat helping.

1 Preheat the oven to 200°C/400°F/gas mark 6.

2 Heat a large saucepan or frying pan with a lid until hot. Add the oil and lamb and fry for 3–4 minutes until browned, stirring occasionally to break up any clumps of meat.

3 When the meat is browned, push it to one side of the pan and add the onion and garlic to the other side. Turn down the heat and sweat the veg gently for 10 minutes, until the onion has softened and just coloured.

4 Mix the lamb and onions together in the pan and add the carrots, red lentils, ketchup, tinned tomatoes and stock. Bring to the boil, stir well then reduce the heat to a simmer. Cover and cook for 20 minutes.

5 While the sauce cooks, start making the topping. Put the potatoes into a medium saucepan and pour over enough boiling water to just cover them. Bring to the boil then reduce the heat and simmer for 15–20 minutes until they are tender – check the potatoes by piercing them with a fork.

6 While the potatoes are cooking, heat the milk in a small saucepan until hot.

7 Drain the cooked potatoes really well then return them to the saucepan and place on the heat for 1 minute to steam and drive off any extra moisture.

8 Add the hot milk and the butter and beat/mash the potatoes until they are smooth. Season to taste with salt and black pepper.

9 When the meat is tender and the sauce has reduced and thickened, remove from the heat, add the parsley and season to taste.

10 Tip the sauce into a large ovenproof dish then spoon the mashed potato on top. Spread the mash gently over the top to evenly cover the meat.

11 Bake in the oven for 20 minutes until golden and bubbling. Serve topped with a little more parsley, if you fancy it.

Bean and vegetable stew

SERVES 8

1 tbsp olive oil

1 onion, finely diced

2 leeks, split lengthways
up to the root several
times, washed under cold
running water then thickly
sliced

2 carrots, peeled and cut into
1cm dice

2 garlic cloves, finely diced

1 tsp smoked paprika

½ tsp dried thyme

2 potatoes, peeled and cut
into 1cm dice

1 litre vegetable stock

½ head cauliflower, cut into
small florets

200g fine green beans, cut
into 2cm pieces

400g tin baked beans

2 tbsp flat-leaf parsley,
roughly chopped

sea salt and freshly ground
black pepper, to taste

crusty bread, to serve

This is a really simple, healthy stew that cooks in just under 30 minutes. The knack to perfectly cooked vegetables throughout is to add them in the correct order – the hardest ones, which are the ones that take the longest cooking first, then onto the green ones, that take the least, so adding the beans at the end.

1 Heat a large frying pan or saucepan until medium hot, add the oil, onion and leeks and sweat for 5 minutes until just softened.

2 Add the carrots, garlic, sweet paprika and dried thyme and stir to combine, then sweat for another 5 minutes.

3 Add the potatoes and vegetable stock and bring to the boil. Turn the heat down and simmer for 5 minutes until the potatoes are just softening then add the cauliflower and simmer for another 5 minutes.

4 By now, all the vegetables should be nearly cooked. Add the green beans and baked beans and cook for 3 minutes until the green beans are just tender, then stir in the chopped parsley and season well with salt and black pepper.

5 Serve hot with plenty of crusty bread.

Tips

- You can add broccoli or any veg that takes your fancy to this – just add the harder veg at the beginning and any softer green veg towards the end. Frozen peas or sweetcorn can also be added at the last minute. Adding baked beans adds a little sweetness and some protein.
- You can also adjust the seasoning/spiciness at the end – add some chilli sauce or flaked chillies for those that like the heat. There are a variety of chilli sauces or chilli pastes available that don't need to be cooked and which can just be added as a condiment. When the stew is ready, spoon out any portions for people that don't like the extra spiciness then adjust the remaining stew. Using smoked sweet paprika to start with gives a little heat and flavour for those who are just getting used to spicy flavours.

Chicken and green bean casserole

SERVES 5

1 tbsp rapeseed oil
5 chicken thigh fillets, skin on
2 large onions, finely chopped
4 garlic cloves
1 tbsp paprika
pinch of cayenne pepper
140g tomato purée
3 carrots, peeled and thickly
    sliced
600g sweet potatoes, washed
    and cut into chunks
2 x 400g tins chopped
    tomatoes
500g long green beans,
    trimmed and cut in 3cm
    lengths
sea salt and freshly ground
    black pepper, to taste

Chicken thighs are packed full of flavour, and sealing them first in the pan before adding all the vegetables means you don't let any of that flavour go to waste.

1 Heat a large casserole or frying pan until hot, add the oil and chicken fillets, flesh side down, and fry until golden on each side. Remove and set aside on a plate.

2 Add the onions to the pan and stir well, scraping up any chicken bits from the bottom of the pan, then turn the heat down and sweat for 5 minutes until just softened.

3 Add the garlic, paprika and cayenne and cook for another minute, then stir in the tomato purée and mix well. Cook for another minute then add the carrots and sweet potatoes and stir really well to coat in the tomato mixture.

4 Add the tinned tomatoes and return the chicken thighs to the pan, then add just enough water so that the chicken and vegetables are all submerged in liquid.

5 Bring to the boil, then turn the heat down to a simmer and cook for 20 25 minutes until the vegetables are tender and the chicken is cooked through. Add the green beans for the last 5 minutes of the cooking time and cook until just tender. Season to taste with a little salt and black pepper.

Puy lentil bolognese with pasta

SERVES 4, WITH ENOUGH
FOR ANOTHER MEAL

1 tbsp olive oil

2 large onions, chopped

3 carrots, peeled and chopped

2 celery sticks, chopped

2 tsp picked thyme leaves or
   1 tsp dried thyme

2 garlic cloves, finely chopped

2 tbsp tomato purée

500g Puy lentils, rinsed and
   drained

400g tin tomatoes

1.5 litres vegetable stock

1 tbsp balsamic vinegar

300g pasta

sea salt and freshly ground
   black pepper, to taste

grated vegetarian cheese, to
   serve

green salad, to serve

A classic ragu, this is great if you want to cut down on your red meat intake – it has all the flavours and textures of a meat ragu.

1 Heat a large frying pan or flameproof casserole dish until medium hot. Add the olive oil, onions, carrots and celery and cook over a medium heat for 5 minutes. You want the veg to soften but not colour – if you like you can put a lid onto the pan to help keep the moisture in and steam the vegetables at the same time.

2 Add the thyme and garlic and cook for another minute, then stir in the tomato purée and turn up the heat. Stir well so that the tomato purée goes all through the vegetables then add the Puy lentils and mix again.

3 Tip in the tinned tomatoes and the vegetable stock, stir well and bring to the boil. Turn the heat down to a gentle simmer and cook for 20–25 minutes until the lentils are tender and the sauce has reduced slightly.

4 Add the balsamic vinegar and season to taste.

5 When the sauce has only 15 minutes left to cook, bring a large saucepan of salted water to the boil. Add the pasta and cook according to the packet instructions until al dente, then drain, reserving some of the cooking water.

6 To serve, remove half the sauce and set aside in a bowl (see page 41).

7 Tip the drained pasta into the pan with the remaining sauce and mix well, adding the reserved pasta water if needed to loosen the sauce and to coat all the pasta.

8 Serve straightaway with a grating of cheese and perhaps a green salad.

Speedy bolognese

1 tsp rapeseed oil
500g minced beef
2 garlic cloves, crushed or
   chopped
3 tbsp tomato purée
1 courgette, cut into small
   dice
1 carrot, peeled and cut into
   small dice
400g passata
150ml beef stock
1 tsp dried basil
1 tsp caster sugar
½ tsp freshly ground
   black pepper
pinch of sea salt
400g spaghetti
finely grated Parmesan
   cheese, to serve

Great for when you only have a little time, this bolognese can be
used for lasagne, cottage pie or jacket potatoes as well.

1 Heat a large frying pan until hot, add the oil and the beef and
fry the meat for about 5 minutes until browned.
2 Add the garlic and purée and cook for another 2 minutes,
stirring well.
3 Add the courgette and carrot and fry for another 2 minutes, then
add the passata, beef stock and basil. Bring to the boil, then lower
the heat and simmer for 10 minutes until the meat is tender and
the sauce has reduced.
4 Add the sugar and season with the black pepper and a pinch of
sea salt.
5 While the sauce is simmering, cook the pasta according to the
packet instructions.
6 Drain the pasta, reserving a spoonful of the pasta water, then
toss the pasta and reserved water into the sauce and cook it for
another minute. Season to taste with more salt and black pepper
and serve with a grating of Parmesan.

Top tips for bolognese

- Cut all the veg the same size so that the dish cooks through evenly.
- Cover the pan with a lid while frying the veg to help the veg soften.
- Only add garlic after everything else has softened so it doesn't burn.
- Reserve some of the cooking water from the pasta to add to the sauce to get a smooth consistency.
- Always add the pasta to the sauce, not the other way around, and finish cooking the pasta in the sauce.
- Divide the remaining sauce into 4 – you can get 4 further meal portions from a batch made from our recipe. Transfer to a freezerproof container, cool, then place in the fridge or the freezer until needed. To serve, simply defrost and reheat.
- Serve one portion with a jacket potato and a dollop of cream cheese.
- Add chilli sauce and tinned kidney beans to make a chilli and serve with rice.
- Layer up the sauce between sheets of lasagne and make a bechamel sauce to serve between the layers to make lasagne.
- Top with a layer of mashed potato and a grating of cheese for a Cumberland pie.

For the puy lentil bolognese...

Adding balsamic at the end gives a little richness and depth of flavour. Extra tip: take a bottle of balsamic vinegar, pour it into a pan and simmer over a medium heat until reduced by half, then decant back into the bottle. You will have a rich, sweet, savoury condiment to add to stews, bologneses, etc. at the end of cooking.

For the speedy bolognese...

You can add a glass of leftover red wine to the sauce after the beef has been browned – this will make the sauce even richer.

Tips

- Chop all the veg while the chicken marinates and the noodles cook – this saves time and means that everything is ready when you start stir-frying.
- Draining and refreshing (running the noodles under cold water) can be done to noodles, rice and pasta if you're making a large batch to use later – it stops the cooking process so that you can just heat them through when needed. Adding a little oil stops them sticking together – you can do this with noodles or pasta (not rice) and by using sesame oil it adds flavour, too.
- Start cooking the ingredients that take the longest to cook (like the chicken), then add the other ingredients in turn, finishing with the one that takes the least amount of time.
- Adding a tiny touch of cornflour thickens the sauce slightly.
- This can be transferred to a sealed container and kept cool in a fridge then reheated in a microwave, but it cannot be frozen.

Chicken satay noodles

SERVES 3

300g chicken or turkey
   breast, cut into strips
2 tbsp soy sauce
½ tsp cornflour
125g dried egg noodles
4 tsp rapeseed oil
3 spring onions, thinly sliced
1–2 hot red chillies, finely
   sliced
2 tbsp peanut butter
2 tbsp sweet chilli sauce
200ml tin reduced-fat
   coconut milk
50g sugar snap peas
100g mixed frozen peas and
   beans
75g frozen sweetcorn
juice of 1 lime
1 carrot, peeled, then cut with
   a peeler into thin slices
40g spinach leaves

To serve
1 tbsp roughly chopped
   cashew nuts
1 tbsp roughly chopped
   coriander sprigs
1 mild red chilli, finely sliced

Poaching the chicken in the sauce here gives a lovely soft texture to the chicken and by adding the carrots and spinach at the end, then turning the heat off, it means you still have perfectly cooked veg with a little bite.

1 Put the chicken or turkey into a bowl with the soy sauce and cornflour and mix well. Set aside while you prepare the noodles.
2 Bring a large pan of water to the boil, add the noodles and cook according to the packet instructions. Tip into a colander and leave to drain. Run cold water through the noodles until they are cold, then drain once more and tip them back into the cold saucepan. Add half the rapeseed oil, toss to combine then set aside – you don't want the noodles to carry on cooking or stick together while you prepare the rest of the dish.
3 Heat a wok until hot, add the remaining rapeseed oil, spring onions and hot chillies and stir-fry for 1 minute until softened.
4 Add the peanut butter, chilli sauce and coconut milk and stir together until they are all combined. Bring to a simmer then add the chicken and poach for 4 minutes until just cooked through. Add 100ml of water to the sauce and return to the boil.
5 Add the sugar snaps and simmer for another 2 minutes until nearly tender, then add the frozen peas, beans and sweetcorn.
6 Return to the boil, then stir in the lime juice and check the seasoning – you might want to add more lime juice or chilli, depending how hot you like it!
7 Stir through the cooked noodles and heat for 1–2 minutes until hot through then finally stir in the carrot peelings and spinach and remove from the heat. The heat from the dish will wilt the spinach down, just stir through a couple of times.
8 Serve with the chopped cashews, coriander and mild red chilli on top.

Spiced chicken with roasted vegetable rice

SERVES 5

4 tbsp olive oil

2 tsp smoked paprika

2 tsp dried basil

1 tsp cayenne pepper

5 boneless, skinless chicken breasts

5 whole garlic cloves, peeled

2 red pepper, deseeded and roughly chopped

1 courgette, roughly chopped

2 onions, roughly chopped

375g long-grain rice

½ x 280g jar sundried tomatoes, drained and roughly chopped

sea salt and freshly ground black pepper, to taste

Cooking the chicken in its own little parcel means that it keeps it very succulent – a perfect accompaniment to the roasted vegetables. Keep any leftover roasted vegetables to throw into an omelette or toss through pasta – they're a great stand-by.

1 Preheat the oven to 200°C/400°F/gas mark 6. Cut 5 pieces of foil each big enough to wrap a chicken breast 1½ times over.

2 Put 2 tablespoons of the olive oil into a small bowl or cup, add the smoked paprika, dried basil and cayenne pepper and mix well.

3 Place a chicken breast onto the centre of each piece of foil, divide the spiced oil among the parcels and turn the chicken in the oil to coat completely. Add a garlic clove to each one, then fold the foil up around the chicken to make a parcel, sealing it well.

4 Put the parcels onto a baking tray and place in the oven for 20 minutes until cooked through.

5 Pile the chopped peppers, courgette and onions into a roasting tin, add the remaining oil and season with salt and black pepper. Toss together then roast in the oven with the chicken.

6 Bring a large saucepan of water to the boil. Meanwhile, rinse the rice in cold water and drain well. Tip the drained rice into the boiling water, stir well then simmer for 15–18 minutes until cooked through. After 15 minutes of cooking, lift a spoonful of rice out of the pan, drain off the water and taste it – if it's cooked there will be no chalkiness in the centre. If there is a tiny white mark in the centre of the grain, it needs to cook for another couple of minutes.

7 Drain the rice into a colander and leave to steam while you get the chicken and vegetables out of the oven. Open the foil parcels, being careful to avoid escaping steam as you do. Check the chicken is cooked by piercing the centre of the chicken with a sharp knife. Don't cut it in half, just slide the knife in, then out again. Any juices coming out should be clear and the tip of the knife should be very hot. If not, return to the oven for another 5 minutes and check again.

8 Tip the cooked rice onto the tray of roasted vegetables and toss together. Add the sundried tomatoes and toss once to mix thoroughly, then season to taste.

9 Serve the chicken on a bed of the roasted vegetable rice with a salad garnish, if you fancy it.

Chips three ways

Chips are a family favourite but you can have healthier chips – they don't need to be deep-fried. Here are three different ways to make the humble chip…

SERVES 4

2 large or 3 medium sweet
   potatoes, scrubbed
4 tsp rapeseed oil
½ tsp chilli powder
½ tsp ground cumin
½ tsp ground coriander
sea salt and freshly ground
   black pepper, to taste

Potato wedges

1 Preheat the oven to 200°C/400°F/gas mark 6.
2 Cut the potatoes in half lengthways and then again into 4–6 wedges, depending on the size of the potatoes.
3 Pour the oil onto a large roasting tin, add the spices and a generous pinch of salt and black pepper and mix together.
4 Toss the potato wedges in the spiced oil until they are fully coated then roast in the oven for 15–20 minutes until browned at the edges and cooked through.
5 Transfer to a plate lined with kitchen paper to remove any excess oil, then serve straightaway.

SERVES 4

2 large or 3 medium King
   Edward potatoes,
   scrubbed and cut into
   1cm wide chips
4 tsp rapeseed oil
sea salt and freshly ground
   black pepper, to taste

Oven chips

1 Preheat the oven to 220°C/425°F/gas mark 7.
2 Place the chips in a saucepan and pour over enough cold water to just cover them. Bring to the boil and simmer for 5 minutes until just tender but still firm. This means they will be cooked through and slightly fluffy in the middle but crispy on the outside.
3 Drain the chips carefully and tip them out onto a sheet of kitchen paper or a tea towel and pat dry.
4 Pour the oil onto a large roasting tray, season with salt and black pepper then add the potatoes and toss them gently in the oil until they are fully coated.
5 Cook in the oven for 15–20 minutes until golden brown, crispy and cooked through.
6 Transfer to a plate lined with kitchen paper to remove any excess oil, then serve straightway.

500g cooked cold new
    potatoes
4 tsp rapeseed oil
sea salt and freshly ground
    black pepper, to taste

Leftover chips

1 Cut the potatoes into even-sized pieces – whichever shape fits the potato, but they need to be able to cook at the same speed in the pan.

2 Heat a large frying pan until hot, add the rapeseed oil and the potatoes and fry on each side for 1–2 minutes until golden brown, crispy and hot through.

3 Transfer to a plate lined with kitchen paper to remove any excess oil, then serve straightway.

Tip
You can add chopped fresh rosemary or thyme, chilli flakes, lemon zest, smoked paprika or even a little curry powder to the potatoes as they fry and crisp up.

Salmon fishcakes

SERVES 6

675g floury potatoes, peeled
    and cut into chunks
500g boneless, skinless
    salmon fillets (about
    4 fillets)
1 tbsp tomato ketchup
1½ tsp English mustard
zest of 1 lemon, chopped into
    wedges to serve
1½ heaped tbsp chopped
    parsley
1½ heaped tbsp chopped dill
4½ tbsp plain flour
2 eggs, beaten
150g dried breadcrumbs
6 tbsp sunflower oil
sea salt and freshly ground
    black pepper, to taste
mixed salad leaves, to serve

If you have any leftover mash you can also use it to make these delicious fish cakes – just be careful to keep some nice big pieces of salmon when you mix it all together.

1 Heat the grill to high.

2 Put the potatoes into a large saucepan and pour over enough cold water to just cover – only add enough water to cover as it takes longer when you overfill. Bring to the boil, then reduce the heat and simmer for 12–15 minutes until tender.

3 While the potatoes cook, grill the salmon. Place the salmon fillets under the grill and cook for 3–4 minutes on each side until just cooked through. Remove and set aside to cool slightly.

4 Drain the potatoes and return them to the saucepan. Set over the heat for 1 minute to drive off any excess moisture left in the potato. Mash the potatoes until smooth then add the ketchup, mustard, lemon zest, parsley and dill and mix really well. Add plenty of salt and black pepper, then mix once more.

5 Flake the salmon into large pieces then fold into the mashed potato, taking care to keep the pieces as big as possible.

6 Divide the mixture into 6 then form each piece into a large patty.

7 Put the flour, eggs and breadcrumbs in 3 separate shallow dishes. Dip the cakes into the flour first then dust off any excess. Dip them into the beaten egg, making sure they're totally covered, then finally dip them into the breadcrumbs to evenly coat.

8 Heat a large frying pan until medium hot, add the oil and the fishcakes and fry gently on each side for 3–4 minutes until deep golden brown and hot all the way through.

9 Serve with salad and lemon wedges for squeezing over.

Tips
- Don't add butter, oil or milk to the mashed potatoes as it can make it too soft and difficult to handle.
- Try using different types of fish – tinned tuna or tinned salmon will also work well. You can use leftover cooked fish here, too.

Lasagne

4 tsp olive oil
250g beef mince or meat-free
    mince
1 onion, diced
2 carrots, peeled and finely
    diced
1 celery stick, finely diced
2 garlic cloves, crushed
½ tsp dried thyme
1 tbsp tomato purée
2 x 400g tins tomatoes
75g butter
75g plain flour
1 tsp English mustard
700ml milk
250g lasagne sheets
100g Cheddar cheese, grated
sea salt and freshly ground
    black pepper, to taste

Tip

You can make this all in
advance and assemble it
when needed – it will take
40–45 minutes to cook
from cold.

Lasagne is many people's favourite dish – here's how to make it
properly. If you don't have the time to make the white sauce, you
can just layer in natural cottage cheese instead.

1 Preheat the oven to 200°C/400°F/gas mark 6.

2 Heat a large frying pan until hot, add 2 teaspoons of the olive oil
and the mince and fry the meat until browned all over. Tip into a
colander set over a bowl, or in the sink, to allow all the fat to drain off.

3 Add the remaining olive oil, the onion, carrots and celery to the
pan, mix well then cover with a lid and fry over a medium heat for
5–8 minutes until just softened.

4 Stir in the garlic, dried thyme and tomato purée and mix well,
then fry for another minute.

5 Add the tinned tomatoes, stirring them all the way through the
mixture, then bring to the boil.

6 Reduce the heat and simmer for 15 minutes until the meat is
tender and the sauce reduced slightly. Season to taste with salt
and black pepper.

7 Meanwhile, heat a medium saucepan until hot, add the butter
and flour and cook together, stirring all the time until it forms a soft
golden paste.

8 Cook for another minute or so, taking care not to let it get too
brown – you are cooking out the flour so you don't have a floury
taste to your sauce.

9 Stir in the mustard, then whisk in the milk, a little at a time,
until you have a thick paste, then add the remainder of the milk,
whisking all the time until you have a smooth sauce. It's much
easier to do it with a whisk than a spoon!

10 Bring to a simmer and cook gently, stirring occasionally, for
another 5 minutes until just thickened. Season to taste with salt
and plenty of black pepper.

11 Now for the assembly – take a large ovenproof dish and layer
in enough of the meat sauce to cover the bottom of the dish. Cover
with a layer of lasagne sheets then top with enough white sauce to
cover. Repeat the layers using up all the sauce, pasta and white
sauce, making sure you finish with the layer of white sauce.

12 Top with the grated cheese then bake in the oven for 30 minutes
until golden brown and bubbling.

Lighter carbonara

SERVES 2 ADULTS,
   3 CHILDREN

400g spaghetti
1 tbsp olive oil
155g smoked diced bacon
2 garlic cloves, finely chopped
   or grated
¼ tsp dried basil
200g frozen peas
1 egg
60ml semi-skimmed milk
50g parmesan or mature
   cheddar cheese, grated
sea salt and freshly ground
   black pepper, to taste

The trick to making a great carbonara is to trust that the eggs will cook in the heat of the pasta. Make sure that the pasta and pea mixture is boiling hot before you tip in the egg – it will instantly cook the egg, and give you a scrambled egg-free carbonara!

1 Bring a large pan of water to the boil. Add a generous pinch of salt with the pasta. Cook the pasta according to packet instructions – set a timer on your phone as a reminder! The salt is just for cooking the pasta, it doesn't count towards your salt content for the day and you definitely don't need any oil in the water – it will stream straight off the pasta as it comes out of the water so it's just wasted.
2 While the pasta cooks, make the sauce. Heat a large frying pan until hot. Add half the oil to the pan along with the diced bacon. Fry for about 3 minutes until it is cooked through and crispy around the edges.
3 Add the rest of the olive oil, the garlic and basil and fry for another minute.
4 Add the frozen peas and cook for 2 more minutes, or until any excess water has boiled off. While you are waiting, crack the egg into a cup, add the milk and whisk with a fork, then put to one side.
5 When the pasta has cooked, drain it into a colander or sieve then set it back over the saucepan to collect a little of the cooking water.
6 Turn the heat off under the pea mixture and toss in the pasta, stirring well so that it is all combined.
7 Immediately add the egg mixture and toss really well to coat. The heat from the pasta will instantly cook the egg so there is no need to turn the heat back on.
8 Stir in the cheese, making sure it goes all the way through, then season well with salt and black pepper. If the mixture is a little dry, add the reserved pasta water and stir through really well. Check the seasoning again and serve straightaway.

Meat-free chilli

SERVES 4

1 tbsp rapeseed oil
1 large onion, finely chopped
2 garlic cloves, finely chopped
1 red chilli, finely chopped
½ tsp ground cumin
1 tbsp paprika
1 tsp chilli powder
250g soya mince
400g tin chopped tomatoes
3 tbsp tomato purée
300ml vegetable stock
1 green pepper, deseeded and
    cut into large dice
1 yellow pepper, deseeded
    and cut into large dice
1 carrot, peeled and grated
400g tin kidney beans in
    water, drained
1 tsp cornflour
handful of coriander, finely
    chopped
sea salt and freshly ground
    black pepper, to taste

To serve
2 wholemeal pitta breads,
    halved
4 tbsp sour cream
50g Cheddar, grated

Everyone likes their chilli at a different heat – add more chillies to start if everyone likes it hot, but if not, add chilli sauce to an individual portion at the end. There are a huge variety available now in the supermarkets – find your favourite one and no longer will the kids say it's too hot for them!

1 Heat a large frying pan until medium hot, then add the oil, onion and garlic and cook for 4–5 minutes, or until just soft.
2 Stir in the red chilli, ground cumin, paprika and chilli powder and cook for 1 minute. Add the soya mince and cook for another 2–3 minutes.
3 Add the chopped tomatoes, tomato purée, stock, peppers and carrot and bring to the boil. Reduce the heat to medium-low and simmer for 10 minutes, stirring occasionally.
4 Add the kidney beans and cook for 5 minutes. Mix the cornflour with 1 tablespoon water in a small bowl, then add it to the pan and cook for a further 5 minutes until the sauce has thickened.
5 Stir in the coriander and season to taste with the sea salt and black pepper.
6 Serve the chilli with the pitta halves, sour cream and grated Cheddar cheese.

Tip
Rather than drinking squash or soft drinks tonight, put some ice cubes in a jug, squeeze in the juice of a whole lemon and lime (chucking the pieces in when they've been squeezed) and top with sparkling water.

Meatballs

SERVES 4

400g lean lamb mince
1 egg, beaten
2 small onions, roughly
    chopped
85g breadcrumbs
1 tbsp finely chopped mint,
    plus extra to serve
4 tsp olive oil
1 tsp tomato purée
½ tsp dried chilli flakes
½ tsp smoked sweet paprika
400g tin chopped tomatoes
300g spaghetti
sea salt and freshly ground
    black pepper, to taste
finely grated Parmesan
    cheese, to serve (optional)

You can make meatballs with any mince you fancy – these are lamb and mint, but you can use beef, pork or even chicken and turkey mince with whichever herbs you have to hand. Make the meatballs spicy with some chilli and garlic or perhaps fruity with some dried cranberries.

1 Put the lamb mince, egg, 1 of the chopped onions, the breadcrumbs and mint into a large bowl and mix really well. Season with salt and black pepper then mix once more and divide in half.

2 Divide each half in half again, then into 5 pieces – you will have 20 pieces of mince. This way you will make all the balls a similar size. Roll the mixture into balls and set aside.

3 Heat a frying pan until medium hot, add 2 teaspoons of the olive oil and the remaining chopped onion and cook for 4–5 minutes until just softened. You can cover the pan with a lid, turn the heat down low and let the onion sweat until it is softened.

4 Meanwhile, heat another frying pan until hot, add the remaining oil and brown the meatballs on each side until golden all over.

5 Remove the lid from the frying pan with the onion, add the tomato purée, chilli flakes and smoked paprika and fry for 1 minute, then add the chopped tomatoes. Half-fill the empty tin with cold water and add to the pan. Bring to a simmer then add the browned meatballs. Cook over a gentle heat for 15 minutes until the meatballs are cooked through and the sauce has reduced slightly. Season with salt and black pepper.

6 While the sauce cooks, bring a large saucepan of salted water to the boil. Add the pasta and cook according to the packet instructions until al dente. Drain the pasta, reserving about 3–4 tablespoons of the cooking water, then add the pasta and reserved water to the sauce. Stir well to coat then cook for another couple of minutes.

7 Serve straightaway – with a grating of Parmesan on top if you fancy it.

Tuna and veg pasta bake

SERVES 4

300g pasta shapes – whatever shape you fancy
150g frozen peas
1 courgette, quartered lengthways and finely chopped
40g butter, diced
40g plain flour
600ml semi-skimmed milk
100g mature Cheddar cheese, grated
160g tin tuna
2 salad tomatoes, sliced
sea salt and freshly ground black pepper, to taste

This is a creamy pasta bake with a classic cheese sauce – finishing it under the grill gives a lovely grilled cheese flavour to go with the flaked tuna.

1 Bring a large saucepan of water to the boil. Add a generous pinch of salt and the pasta. Cook the pasta according to packet instructions until al dente – set a timer on your phone as a reminder! You definitely don't need any oil in the water for cooking the pasta. The oil will stream straight off of the pasta as it comes out of the water so it's a waste.

2 About 2 minutes before the pasta is ready, add the frozen peas and chopped courgette to the pan and cook together for 2 minutes until the pasta is cooked through and the courgette is just tender.

3 While the pasta is cooking, put the butter, flour and milk into a medium saucepan and set over a medium heat. Bring to the boil, whisking all the time, until the mixture thickens to a sauce consistency – it should just be thick enough to coat the back of a spoon. Dip a spoon into the sauce, then lift it out and carefully draw a finger in a line down the back of it – the sauce should stay on the spoon with a clean line down the centre.

4 Stir half the cheese into the sauce and season with the salt and black pepper. Return to the heat, stirring occasionally, until the cheese has melted.

5 Preheat the grill and place a shallow, ovenproof dish underneath to warm up.

6 When the pasta and vegetables are cooked, drain them into a colander or sieve then tip into the warmed ovenproof dish and flake the tuna over the top.

7 Spoon the cheese sauce over the tuna then decorate with the sliced tomatoes and finish with the last of the grated cheese and some seasoning.

8 Place under the grill until the cheese has melted and started to go golden (roughly 4–5 minutes). Serve straightaway.

Asian chicken with rice and broccoli

3 tbsp soy sauce

4 tsp rapeseed oil

2 tbsp honey

1 tsp finely grated fresh root ginger

1 tsp finely chopped or grated garlic

2 boneless, skinless chicken breasts

150g long-grain rice

2 spring onions, roughly chopped

1/3 broccoli head, cut into florets and thinly sliced

A quick stir-fry dinner for when you want something spicy and nutritious but quickly.

1 In a bowl big enough to fit the chicken breasts in, combine the soy sauce, 3 teaspoons of the oil, the honey, ginger and garlic. Add the chicken breasts and toss to coat thoroughly in the marinade. Cover the bowl with cling film and place in the fridge for at least 15 minutes to marinate.

2 Meanwhile, put the rice in a sieve under cold running water, drain, then tip into a medium saucepan. Pour over 350ml of cold water and stir well. Place on the heat and bring to the boil. When the water is boiling, reduce the heat so the water just simmers, then cover with a lid. Cook gently for 15–18 minutes, or until tender and all the water is absorbed. Lift the lid and you will see small dimples in the rice – this is an indicator that all the water is absorbed. Test a grain or two of rice, it should be tender. Take the rice off the heat and gently run a fork through it to separate the rice grains.

3 Towards the end of the rice cooking time, preheat the grill to medium-high. Remove the chicken from the marinade, but reserve the marinade.

4 Lightly oil the grill grate and cook the chicken for 6–8 minutes on each side, brushing frequently with the reserved marinade. To see if the chicken is cooked, pierce the thickest part of it with a sharp knife – don't cut it in half, just slide the knife in, then out again. Any juices coming out should run clear and the tip of the knife should be very hot. If not, return to the grill for another 2–3 minutes on each side.

5 Just before you are ready to serve, heat a frying pan until hot, then add the remaining teaspoon of oil and the spring onions and broccoli. Stir-fry for a couple of minutes until just softened then tip in the cooked rice and stir to combine.

6 Divide the broccoli rice between the plates and serve the chicken alongside.

Tuna burgers

SERVES 8

2 x 340g tins tuna in water,
    drained
100g fresh breadcrumbs
2 eggs, beaten
4 tbsp mayonnaise
4 spring onions, finely
    chopped
1 garlic clove, finely chopped
    or grated
2 tsp vegetable oil, for frying
sea salt and freshly ground
    black pepper, to taste

Tuna mayonnaise in a burger form, what more can you want from a tuna burger? These are great and a little goes a long way.

1 Mix all the ingredients except the vegetable oil together in a large bowl, until they form a smooth paste.

2 Season with salt and black pepper then divide into 8. Form each eighth into a burger shape then set side.

3 Heat a frying pan until medium hot. Add the vegetable oil and fry the burgers, in 2 batches if needed, on each side for 2 minutes until just golden brown and hot through. Check that each is hot by inserting a knife into the burger and holding for 2 seconds, then removing and checking to see if it is piping hot. If not, continue to cook for another 2 minutes.

Pork and apple burgers

SERVES 4, WITH ENOUGH
FOR ANOTHER MEAL

750g pork mince

75g fresh breadcrumbs

2 level tsp fresh sage, finely
    chopped or 1 tsp dried
    sage

1 dessert apple, coarsely
    grated

2 spring onions, finely
    chopped

1 egg, lightly beaten

1 tsp olive oil

sea salt and freshly ground
    black pepper, to taste

To serve

4 burger buns, split

1-2 tbsp English mustard, to
    taste

1 head Little Gem lettuce,
    leaves separated

2 tomatoes, thickly sliced

½ small red onion, cut into
    rings

The apple and breadcrumbs added to the pork mince make this
a really soft-textured juicy burger. You can make the burgers in
advance and leave them in the fridge until ready to cook.

1 Preheat the oven to 190°C/375°F/gas mark 5 and line a baking
tray with tin foil.

2 Place all the burger ingredients except the olive oil into a bowl
with a good pinch of salt and black pepper. Mix really well until
combined; start with a spoon then finish with your hands to get it
really well mixed.

3 Divide the mixture in half. Place one half into a bowl or box,
cover and place in the fridge until needed – it should be used
within 2 days. Divide the rest into 4 and form into patties.

4 Heat a frying pan until medium hot, then add the burgers and
fry on each side for 45-60 seconds until just browned. Lift out and
place onto the lined baking tray. Bake in the oven for 15 minutes
until cooked through and hot. To check that the burgers are
cooked, insert the tip of a sharp knife into the centre of one. If it
comes out hot, the burger is cooked, if it isn't, return to the oven
for a further 5 minutes.

5 While the burgers cook, spread the buns with as much mustard
as you fancy, then layer up with the burgers, the lettuce, tomatoes
and onion rings.

Homemade burgers

400g tin kidney beans,
    drained and rinsed
3 tbsp vegetable oil
1 onion, finely chopped
1 large carrot, peeled and
    grated
1 tsp ground cumin
1 spring onion, finely chopped
1 garlic clove, crushed or
    finely grated
1 tbsp flat leaf parsley, finely
    chopped
1 heaped tsp plain flour,
    plus another to shape the
    burgers

To serve
4 burger buns, split
½ iceberg lettuce, leaves
    shredded
4 tomatoes, quartered
1 yellow pepper, deseeded
    and sliced
1 green pepper, deseeded and
    sliced
1 tsp balsamic vinegar
1 tbsp olive oil
sea salt and freshly ground
    black pepper, to taste

The trick to these is cooking the beans for a little while to soften them, then adding a little flour into the mixture when you bring it all together. If not, you will be left with very crumbly burgers.

1 Tip the drained kidney beans into a saucepan, cover with cold water and bring to the boil. Lower the heat and simmer for about 10 minutes until softened, then drain and set aside.

2 Meanwhile, heat a large frying pan until hot, add 1 tablespoon of the vegetable oil and the onion, carrot, cumin, spring onion and garlic and fry for 3–4 minutes until just softened.

3 Add the drained kidney beans to the frying pan, stir well then remove from the heat.

4 Add the chopped parsley and season well, then mash the mixture together to form a thick paste. Stir in the flour to stiffen the mixture – if not it will fall apart when you try to fry the burgers.

5 Lightly flour your hands and divide the mixture into 4 and form 4 patties, then set them onto a plate.

6 Clean out the large frying pan and return it to the heat. When it is medium hot, add the last of the vegetable oil and start to cook the burgers. Cook for 2–3 minutes on one side, before carefully turning so as not to break them.

7 Keep turning and cooking the burgers on both sides until crisp and hot through.

8 While the burgers cook, toast or griddle the burger buns until warm through. Toss the lettuce, tomatoes and peppers together in a bowl then add the vinegar and olive oil and toss together until coated. Season to taste, then serve the burgers in the buns with the salad alongside.

Tandoori chicken skewers

SERVES 4

75g plain yoghurt
2 tbsp tikka spice curry paste
450g chicken thigh fillets,
    trimmed of fat and each
    one cut into 4 strips
small bunch of coriander,
    chopped
1 lime, cut into wedges

These can be prepared in advance then left to marinate in the fridge while, if the weather's good, you get the barbecue going. You want to make sure the chicken is cooked all the way through so don't press it together too tightly on the skewer.

1 Put the yoghurt and tikka paste into a bowl and mix together. Add the chicken, toss to coat thoroughly, then cover and place into the fridge to marinate for at least 20 minutes, but up to 4 hours.
2 Soak some bamboo skewers in cold water while the chicken marinates – this will stop them burning when you cook the kebabs.
3 Preheat the barbecue or the oven to 220°C/425°F/gas mark 7. Place 2 baking trays in the oven to heat.
4 Pick out a couple of pieces of chicken at a time and thread them onto the soaked skewers, making sure they're not too tightly packed as this will stop them cooking evenly. Place the loaded skewers onto the baking trays.
5 Repeat with the remaining chicken and skewers then barbecue or roast in the oven for 15–20 minutes until the chicken is cooked through. Turn the skewers over halfway through – you may need to tip out some cooking juices from the baking tray so that the skewers brown up nicely and don't poach in the liquid.
6 Lay onto a serving platter, scatter the coriander over, then squeeze the lime over the top and serve straightaway.

Pizza three ways

Pizza is a fab way of using up leftovers! Once you have your base, you can pretty much use any flavour combination you fancy. If you don't have time to make your own bases, these toppings work really well on pitta, naans, flat breads or crumpets. Just top them and heat them through in the oven for 8–10 minutes.

MAKES 3–4 MEDIUM PIZZAS

500g strong bread flour,
    plus extra for dusting
½ tsp salt
1½ tsp caster sugar
7g fast-action dried yeast
½ quantity Tomato and Basil
    Sauce (see page 90) or
    250g passata or
    4 tbsp tomato purée

For a margherita topping
200g mozzarella, thinly sliced
small handful of basil leaves

Tips

Always place your pizza base onto a sheet of baking parchment before you top it otherwise it will just stick to the work surface. Putting baking trays into the oven to heat first means you get a nice crispy base – they would traditionally be cooked on a pizza stone.

1 Tip the flour, salt, sugar and yeast into a large bowl and mix with your hands to combine.

2 Add 325ml water in a steady stream, stirring as you go with a spoon to form a lumpy mass, then get your hands in there. Squeeze the dough together until it becomes smoother, then tip out onto a lightly floured work surface.

3 Knead the dough with your knuckles then pull back with the heel of your hand and repeat. Keep doing this for a good 5 minutes until the dough becomes smooth and pliable – it wants to stretch easily. The longer you knead the dough the better the crust will be!

4 When it's nicely smooth, place into a clean, lightly oiled bowl, cover and set aside to rise for at least 1 hour.

5 When it has risen, you need to knock the air out of it – drop it onto the work surface and knead once more. You can divide the dough into 4 and freeze any portions that you are not using. Cover with cling film or put in a freezer bag and freeze. You can defrost in the fridge over a couple of hours or at room temperature in 1 hour.

6 Preheat the oven as high as it will go and put a couple of large baking sheets onto the oven shelves. Roll each portion of dough out on a lightly dusted work surface into a circle – if you like thin crust, roll to about 5mm thick, if not, then leave it about 1cm thick.

7 Transfer the discs of dough to separate pieces of baking parchment. Spread the tomato sauce over the top of each pizza, then scatter over your chosen toppings – always finish with the cheese so that it melts over the rest of the toppings. Leave any herbs or leaves until the pizza comes out of the oven.

9 Slide a thin board or upturned baking tray under each pizza then scoot it straight onto one of the heated baking trays in the oven. Bake for 10–15 minutes, depending on how hot your oven will go and how thick your dough is. Keep an eye on the pizzas – you want the bases to be cooked through and the toppings to be just perfectly cooked.

10 Remove from the oven and serve straightaway, sliding the pizzas off the baking parchment onto serving plates or a board.

Chickpea crust pizza

240g gram flour (chickpea flour)
pinch of caster sugar
2 garlic cloves, crushed
4 tbsp rapeseed oil

For the topping
4 tbsp tomato purée
1 red onion, finely sliced
1 green pepper, deseeded and diced
250g frozen sweetcorn, defrosted
110g cherry tomatoes, halved
1½ tsp dried oregano
250g mozzarella, drained and thinly sliced
sea salt and freshly ground black pepper, to taste

1 Tip the gram flour into a large bowl with 2 generous pinches of salt and black pepper and a pinch of caster sugar. Add the garlic, 2 tablespoons of the rapeseed oil and 470ml cold water and whisk to a smooth batter. Set aside at room temperature for 1 hour to rest.

2 Preheat the oven to 210°C/410°F/gas mark 7 and lightly grease 2 baking trays.

3 Heat a medium non-stick frying pan until hot, add 1 tablespoon of the rapeseed oil and half the batter. Fry for 3–4 minutes until the batter has bubbled up slightly and is crispy around the edges. Flip over with a fish slice then fry on the other side for another 3–4 minutes – both sides should now be golden brown and the base cooked through.

4 Carefully tip out the base onto one of the baking trays then repeat with the remaining rapeseed oil and batter.

5 Divide the tomato purée between the 2 bases and spread it out to cover them, leaving 1cm clear around the edges. Scatter the vegetables on top then sprinkle the oregano over.

6 Finish with the slices of mozzarella then bake in the oven for 8–10 minutes until golden brown and hot through.

7 Cool slightly before serving half a pizza each.

More toppings

Spanish-style
100g thinly sliced chorizo
150g roast red peppers, sliced
½ red onion, finely sliced
80g green olives
125g Manchego cheese, thinly sliced

Italian-style
300g cooked new potatoes, roughly chopped
250g charred artichokes in oil, drained
200g Gorgonzola cheese
2 tbsp finely grated Parmesan cheese
small handful of rocket

Veggie
4 tbsp pesto (instead of tomato sauce)
2 courgettes, thinly sliced and charred on a griddle
80g frozen spinach
1 red pepper, deseeded and roughly chopped
100g mushrooms, thickly sliced
1 red onion, cut into small wedges
120g frozen sweetcorn, defrosted
basil leaves

Optional extras
drizzle of chilli oil
chilli flakes or chilli sauce
chopped jalapeno peppers
olives
red onion, finely sliced
cherry tomatoes, halved
charred asparagus
sliced salami
Parma ham
cooked ham
cooked bolognese sauce
cooked chicken
grated Cheddar cheese
eggs: crack an egg into the centre of a pizza and bake
basil or mint leaves

Thai salmon and bean curry

For the sauce

1 small onion

3 birds eye chillies, deseeded
and roughly chopped

3 garlic cloves

5cm piece fresh root ginger,
peeled and roughly
chopped

1 tbsp soy sauce

1 tsp ground cumin

1 tsp ground coriander

1 tbsp brown sugar

zest and juice of 2 limes

1 tbsp vegetable oil

400ml tin reduced-fat
coconut milk

For the curry

500g salmon fillet, cut into
small chunks

200g green beans, each cut
into 3 pieces

small handful of basil leaves,
roughly torn

small handful of coriander
leaves, roughly chopped

Thai curry sauces are very simple to make – make a batch then freeze to use when you don't have much time to pull a meal together. Simply heat the sauce and add whatever you fancy – salmon, chicken, beef, tofu to name a few.

1 Start by making the sauce. Place all the ingredients except the oil and the coconut milk into a food processor or blender and blitz to a fine purée. You don't want any texture left at all.

2 Heat a wok until hot, then add the oil to the pan and when it's shimmering, add the paste and cook for 1–2 minutes, stirring all the time. You want to cook the spices but you don't want it to catch.

3 Add the coconut milk and bring to a simmer. Simmer for about 4–5 minutes until the sauce has started to thicken slightly, then taste. You can adjust the sauce at this stage – adding some more soy sauce or lime juice, depending how you like it.

4 If not using straightaway, tip into a large bowl and cool to room temperature before dividing into 4 portions and freezing. This can be kept in the freezer for 3 months. To defrost, leave the sauce in the fridge overnight or put in the microwave on defrost setting until fully defrosted.

5 If reheating, heat a wok until hot, add the sauce and cook until just simmering, stirring occasionally and making sure it doesn't catch on the bottom of the wok.

6 Add the salmon and beans and simmer for 4–5 minutes until the salmon is just cooked through and the beans are tender.

7 Taste the sauce to see if you need to adjust the seasoning at all – again, you can add more soy sauce or lime juice if desired.

8 Stir through the basil and coriander and serve straightaway with some steamed rice.

Sides with a twist

Vegetables can sometimes be a little boring – here are four interesting and tasty ways to pimp them up.

Zesty peas

400g frozen peas
1 tsp olive oil
3 spring onions, finely
    chopped
1 red chilli, finely chopped
small handful of mint leaves,
    finely chopped
zest and juice of ½ lemon
sea salt and freshly ground
    black pepper, to taste

1 Bring a saucepan of water to the boil, add the peas and simmer for 2–3 minutes until hot through. Drain into a colander or sieve and set to one side.
2 Return the empty saucepan to the heat, add the olive oil, spring onions and chilli and fry for 1–2 minutes until just softened.
3 Stir in the peas then turn off the heat. Add the mint, lemon zest and juice and season to taste with salt and black pepper.
4 Finish by bashing the pea mixture with a potato masher – you can make it as crushed or puréed as you like. Serve straightaway.

SERVES 4

Carrots and cumin

4 carrots, peeled and cut
    into chunks
25g butter
1 tbsp sugar
1 tsp ground cumin
sea salt and freshly ground
    black pepper, to taste

1 Put the carrots into a saucepan, add the butter, sugar, cumin and enough water to just cover the carrots.
2 Bring to a simmer over a medium heat, then cover with a lid and simmer for 5–6 minutes until just tender.
3 Remove the lid and cook for another 2 minutes until the carrots are tender and glazed with the liquid. Season with some salt and black pepper.

SERVES 4

Broccoli and chilli

½ head broccoli, stem cut
    into thick slices, the rest
    cut into florets
1 red chilli, finely sliced
2 tsp toasted sesame oil
1 tbsp sesame seeds
sea salt and freshly ground
    black pepper, to taste

1 Bring a pan of water to the boil. Set a colander, sieve or steamer over the top then put the broccoli into it. Cover with a lid and steam for 4–5 minutes until the broccoli is just tender.
2 While the broccoli steams, toss the chilli, sesame oil and sesame seeds together in a bowl big enough to hold the broccoli, then season with salt and black pepper.
3 Lift out the broccoli, tip into the bowl with the chilli and sesame oil and toss to coat.
4 Serve straightaway or chill and serve as a salad.

SERVES 4

Parsnips and honey

4 medium parsnips, peeled
    and cut into quarters
    lengthways
1 tbsp olive oil
2 tbsp honey
sea salt and freshly ground
    black pepper, to taste

1 Preheat the oven to 200°C/400°F/gas mark 6.
2 Tip the parsnips into a roasting tin, drizzle over the olive oil, salt and black pepper and toss to coat.
3 Roast the parsnips for 20 minutes, turning halfway through cooking, then drizzle over the honey and roast for about another 10 minutes until tender and sticky.
4 Serve straightaway.

2 Quick and Simple Suppers

Couscous salad with salmon

SERVES 5

350ml vegetable stock
350g couscous
2 tbsp rapeseed oil
juice of 1 lemon
5 eggs
2 x 212g tins salmon
4 spring onions, finely
    chopped
1 red chilli, finely chopped
150g frozen peas, defrosted
325g tin sweetcorn, drained
large handful of parsley, finely
    chopped
80g baby spinach
sea salt and freshly ground
    black pepper, to taste

A great store cupboard ingredient, couscous is a brilliant vehicle for many flavours – here it's combined with tinned salmon.

1 Bring the stock to the boil and put the couscous into a heatproof bowl. Pour the stock over the couscous then add 1 tablespoon of the rapeseed oil and half the lemon juice. Stir well, then cover with cling film and leave for 10 minutes.
2 Bring a pan of water to the boil, turn down to a simmer and gently lower the eggs into the water. Cook for 8–12 minutes depending on whether you prefer soft- or hard-boiled eggs. Tip off the water and pour over cold water to stop the eggs cooking. Leave to cool slightly.
3 Use a fork to fluff up the couscous. Drain and flake in the salmon, then add the onions, chilli, peas, sweetcorn and most of the parsley. Add the remaining oil and lemon juice, then mix really well and season to taste with salt and black pepper.
4 Shell the cooked eggs and slice into quarters from the top down.
5 Plate the couscous on a bed of baby spinach. Top each portion with an egg, garnish with the remaining parsley and serve.

Smoked salmon, pea and broccoli frittata

SERVES 4

6 eggs
50ml milk
60g smoked salmon
    trimmings
1 tbsp rapeseed oil
¼ head broccoli, cut into
    florets then thinly sliced
100g frozen peas
sea salt and freshly ground
    black pepper, to taste

A cheap yet upmarket and filling way to make a quick meal from half a dozen eggs. If you don't have smoked salmon to hand, you can substitute chicken or ham.

1 Preheat the oven to 200°C/400°F/gas mark 6. Crack the eggs into a large jug and whisk with the milk, a pinch of salt and plenty of black pepper. Add the smoked salmon trimmings and stir well.

2 Heat a medium ovenproof frying pan until just hot, then add a splash of the oil and the broccoli and stir-fry for 3 minutes until just softened. Add the peas and cook for another minute until the peas are just defrosted.

3 Add the remaining oil and give the pan a shake to evenly distribute the vegetables, then turn the heat up high. Pour in the egg mixture and stir briefly, then after a minute turn the hob down to a medium heat.

4 Fry, without stirring, for 2–3 minutes then carefully lift the edge/base of the frittata with a spatula to check if it is cooked and golden underneath. If it isn't, cook for another 1 minute then check again.

5 Pop the entire pan in the oven and bake for 10–12 minutes – when the top is bubbled up and slightly golden use a tea towel to grab the handle and give the pan a gentle shake. If the middle wobbles it needs a little longer; if it's fairly firm, pull it out and put it aside to cool slightly.

6 Slide the frittata out of the pan onto a plate or chopping board. Cut the frittata into slices and serve with some homemade chips (see pages 46–47).

Chorizo and bean stew

SERVES 4

rapeseed oil, for frying
110g cooking chorizo, skin
    peeled off and cut into
    pieces
1 onion, finely chopped
1 garlic clove, crushed
400g tin chopped tomatoes
600g tin cannellini beans in
    water, drained
handful of flat leaf parsley,
    roughly chopped
sea salt and freshly ground
    black pepper, to taste
crusty bread, to serve

A classic combination of chorizo and beans – this packs a spicy
punch and can be made in under 20 minutes.

1 Heat a large lidded saucepan over a medium-low heat. Add the
rapeseed oil and the chorizo and cook until the oil starts to run
from the chorizo.
2 Add the onion and garlic and cook, stirring from time to time,
until soft – cover with a lid to help keep the onion from browning.
3 Add the tomatoes and beans, stir well then cover again and
simmer for 10 minutes. (Add a little water if the stew is too thick.)
4 Stir the parsley into the stew then season to taste with sea salt
and pepper.
5 Serve in soup bowls with some crusty bread.

Haddock chowder

SERVES 8

4 tbsp olive oil
50g butter
2 onions, finely chopped
1 celery stick, roughly
    chopped
100g bacon lardons
4 potatoes, peeled, quartered
    and sliced thickly
2 leeks, split lengthways,
    washed and thickly sliced
600ml fish stock
200ml white wine
1kg undyed smoked haddock,
    skinned and cut into small
    chunks
150g frozen peas
200ml double cream
sea salt and freshly ground
    black pepper, to taste
bunch of flat leaf parsley,
    roughly chopped, to serve
crusty bread, to serve

A traditional creamy chowder is really satisfying to cook and eat
– here's an easy to follow recipe.

1 Heat a large saucepan until medium hot. Add the olive oil and
butter and when it's just foaming, add the onions, celery and
lardons and stir well. Cover with a lid and cook for 5 minutes until
the vegetables are just softened and the bacon is coloured.
2 Add the potatoes and leeks, stir to combine then turn the heat
up slightly. Cover and cook for another 10 minutes.
3 Add the fish stock and wine, stir, and cover once more, then
simmer for 5 minutes. By now the vegetables should all be just
about tender.
4 Add the fish and peas then return to a simmer, cover once more
and cook for another 3 minutes until the fish is cooked through and
the peas are hot.
5 Remove from the heat, stir in the cream and season to taste.
6 Serve with a sprinkling of parsley and some crusty bread.

Tip
You can peel and chop the potatoes in advance then keep
them in a bowl of cold water. You can do this any time you
want to get ahead with potatoes.

Homemade pasta sauces

Homemade pasta sauces are so simple to make, and take very little time, but the end results make shop-bought sauces something you'll not want to go back to. Here are three different ones to get you started.

SERVES 4

Tomato and basil

2 tbsp olive oil
1 onion, finely chopped
1 garlic clove, finely chopped
2 large sprigs of basil, roughly
    chopped
400g tin chopped tomatoes
pinch of caster sugar
sea salt and freshly ground
    black pepper, to taste

1 Heat a frying pan until medium hot. Add the olive oil and onion, cover with a lid and sweat for 5 minutes until softened.
2 Add the garlic and basil and cook for 1 minute then stir in the chopped tomatoes and bring to a simmer.
3 Cook for 5–6 minutes until thickened slightly then season with sugar, salt and black pepper.

SERVES 4

Pesto

large bunch of basil, roughly
    chopped
1 garlic clove, peeled
25g Parmesan cheese, grated
25g pine nuts, toasted
60ml extra virgin olive oil
sea salt and freshly ground
    black pepper, to taste

1 Put the basil, garlic, Parmesan and pine nuts into a food processor and blitz until just broken up.
2 Add the olive oil and continue blitzing until it becomes a slightly chunky paste – you want a little texture but not big pieces of nut left.
3 Season to taste with salt and black pepper. This can be kept, covered, in the fridge for 2–3 days.

2 tbsp olive oil

2 garlic cloves, roughly
  chopped

4 anchovies, roughly chopped

½ tsp chilli flakes (or more if
  you fancy it hot!)

400g cherry tomatoes, roughly
  chopped

2 level tbsp capers, roughly
  chopped

75g green olives, pitted and
  roughly chopped

1 tbsp flat leaf parsley,
  roughly chopped (optional)

sea salt and freshly ground
  black pepper, to taste

Puttanesca

1 Heat a large frying pan until medium-hot, add the olive oil, garlic and anchovies and fry over a gentle heat, stirring occasionally to break up the anchovies. Make sure the pan isn't too hot as you just want to flavour the oil, not burn the garlic!

2 Add the chilli flakes and fry for 30 seconds, then add the cherry tomatoes and cook for 10 minutes, mashing them down slightly with a spoon. You want to release all the juices from the tomatoes into the sauce.

3 Add the capers and olives and cook for another 2 minutes then finish with the parsley, if using, and season to taste with salt and black pepper.

No-pastry quiche

SERVES 6

25g butter, plus extra for
    greasing
6 rashers streaky bacon,
    roughly chopped
6 spring onions, roughly
    chopped
150ml semi-skimmed milk
6 eggs
75g Cheddar cheese, grated
sea salt and freshly ground
    black pepper, to taste

An old-school quiche stands the test of time, but you don't always
have the time to make it. Here's a quick version without the pastry
that should hit the spot.

1 Preheat the oven to 180°C/350°F/gas mark 4. Thoroughly grease
a deep 6-hole bun tin with butter then set aside.

2 Heat a frying pan until hot, add the butter and bacon and fry for
2–3 minutes until just starting to colour, then add the spring onions
and cook for another 2 minutes until softened and the bacon is
cooked through. Remove from the heat and set aside to cool a little.

3 Whisk the milk and eggs together in a large jug then add the
cheese and cooled bacon mixture. Season well with sea salt and
black pepper.

4 Pour into the bun tin, filling each one halfway up, then go round
and top up each one just a little bit so that you don't have some big
and some small.

5 Put into the oven to bake for 15 minutes until golden and risen.
Allow to cool in the tin for 5 minutes before tipping out. Serve the
quiches hot or cold.

Parmesan-crumbed fish

SERVES 5

1 tbsp rapeseed oil
5 x 150g pollock, cod or white
  sustainable fish fillets,
  skinned and boned
60g fresh breadcrumbs
30g Parmesan cheese, finely
  grated
2 tbsp flat leaf parsley, finely
  chopped
zest of 1 lemon
sea salt and freshly ground
  black pepper, to taste

This is like a deconstructed grown-up fish finger – add whatever soft herbs you have to hand and use any white fish.

1 Preheat the oven to 180°C/350°F/gas mark 4.
2 Carefully rub half the oil over the fish then season with sea salt and black pepper. Put onto a baking tray and place in the oven for 10 minutes.
3 While the fish cooks, make the topping. Mix the breadcrumbs, Parmesan, parsley and lemon zest together in a bowl until evenly mixed then season with plenty of black pepper. Add the last of the rapeseed oil and mix through – this will just help it stick together.
4 Remove the fish from the oven and press the breadcrumb mixture onto the top of fillets, taking care not to touch the hot tray!
5 Return to the oven and bake for a further 5–10 minutes, or until the crumbs are light golden and the fish is cooked through.

Cod with warm tomato and olive salsa

SERVES 4

4 x 150–175g skinless cod
    fillets
16 cherry tomatoes, halved
16 black olives, stoned
½ onion, finely chopped
handful of basil leaves,
    roughly chopped
4 tsp rapeseed oil
sea salt and freshly ground
    black pepper, to taste
cooked new potatoes, to serve

Cod with tomatoes and olives is a very Provençal dish and cooking the fish in a parcel, or "en papillote" carries on the traditional French theme, and is a great one to bring to the home kitchen.

1 Preheat the oven to 200°C/400°F/gas mark 6.
2 Take 4 large rectangles of silver foil and place them on the work surface. Put a piece of cod in the centre of each one then divide the tomatoes, olives, onion and basil leaves among the parcels.
3 Pull up the sides of each piece of foil slightly, then drizzle a teaspoon of rapeseed oil over each one. Season with sea salt and black pepper.
4 Pull the foil up around the cod and crimp closed at the top to make a sealed parcel. Transfer to a baking tray and bake in the oven for 15–25 minutes. The cod should be cooked through and the tomatoes softened.
5 Transfer the parcels to serving plates and carefully open up the foil, being careful to avoid escaping steam as you do – serve with some new potatoes.

> **Tip**
> You can do this with any piece of fish you fancy. Making a parcel and cooking it 'en papillotte' is a very French way of cooking and retains all the natural juices in the fish. It also makes it very difficult to overcook the fish.

Roasted tomato, basil and garlic pasta

SERVES 4

8 medium-sized tomatoes, cut
    in half
1 head of garlic, broken up
    but skin left on
100g bacon lardons
1 tbsp rapeseed oil
360g pasta (your favourite
    shape)
1 large handful of basil leaves
2 tbsp extra virgin olive oil
sea salt and freshly ground
    black pepper, to taste
freshly grated Parmesan
    cheese, to serve

Roasting the tomatoes intensifies the flavour and gives a lovely texture to this chunky pasta sauce. You could even serve it with a jacket potato instead of pasta.

1 Preheat the oven to 200°C/400°F/gas mark 6.

2 Place the tomatoes, garlic and bacon in a roasting tray then drizzle over the rapeseed oil and season with salt and black pepper.

3 Toss everything well then roast in the oven for 20 minutes until the tomatoes start to spilt and ooze. Check the tray halfway through cooking to make sure the garlic doesn't burn.

4 Meanwhile, bring a large saucepan of salted water to the boil and add the pasta. Cook according to packet instructions, then drain, reserving some of the cooking water.

5 Tip the roasted tomato mixture into the saucepan used to cook the pasta and give it a good stir so it just starts to break down. Add the drained pasta and a couple of spoonfuls of the pasta water and toss everything together.

6 Tear the basil leaves in to the pasta then serve straightaway, drizzled with the extra virgin olive oil and scattered with Parmesan.

Microwave tomato risotto

SERVES 4

30g butter
1 onion, diced
300g arborio rice
500g passata
1 vegetable stock cube,
    crumbled
300ml cold water
250g salad tomatoes or cherry
    tomatoes, roughly chopped
125g mozzarella, drained and
    grated
sea salt and freshly ground
    black pepper, to taste

Yes, a risotto that's microwaved! It is so simple and means you don't need to stand there stirring the pan for 25 minutes. Just adjust the timings for the power of your microwave.

1 Put the butter, onion and rice into a large heatproof bowl then cover with cling film. Put the bowl into a microwave and cook on high for 3 minutes.
2 Lift the bowl out of the microwave and carefully remove the cling film, watching out for steam escaping.
3 Add the passata, stock cube and water to the bowl and stir really well, then place the bowl back into the microwave, uncovered, and cook on high for a further 10 minutes.
4 Remove the bowl from the microwave again and stir in the chopped tomatoes and grated mozzarella really well to mix the cheese through the risotto.
5 Return the bowl to the microwave one last time and cook for another 8 minutes. Taste to check that the rice and tomatoes are cooked through, then season with salt and black pepper and give the risotto one final big stir before serving.

Tips
Try adding chilli, lemon zest or herbs to the risotto for a change. Any leftover risotto can be made into little balls, then coated in flour, egg and breadcrumbs and deep-fried.

White fish and bacon parcels

SERVES 2 ADULTS,
   2 KIDS

large bunch of basil, roughly
   chopped
1 garlic clove, peeled
25g Parmesan cheese, grated
25g pine nuts, toasted
60ml extra virgin olive oil
500g white fish fillets
   (whatever you have in your
   freezer – cod, pollock and
   monkfish work best)
200g unsmoked bacon
   medallions
1 tbsp rapeseed oil
sea salt and freshly ground
   black pepper, to taste
steamed tenderstem broccoli,
   to serve
boiled crushed new potatoes,
   to serve

You can use any firm white fish to make these, and can wrap them in bacon, thinly sliced pancetta, Parma ham or even chorizo.

1 Put the basil, garlic, Parmesan and pine nuts into a food processor and blitz until just broken up.

2 Add the olive oil and continue blitzing until the mixture becomes a slightly chunky paste – you want a little texture but not big pieces of nut left.

3 Season to taste with salt and black pepper then set aside while you prepare the fish.

4 Cut the fish into thick fingers – about 2cm wide and 8cm long if possible. Cut the bacon medallions in half lengthways then, using the back of the knife, flatten the bacon out lengthways, stretching it as you go. This will make it thin and long enough to wrap around the fish.

5 For the children, simply wrap a strip of bacon around the fish to cover as much of the middle as possible. For the adults, brush the fish with the pesto all over, then wrap up with the bacon in the same way.

6 Heat a frying pan until hot, add the oil and the bacon-wrapped fish join-side down into the pan and fry for 1 minute until the bacon is coloured and the join secure. Flip over and cook on each side for 1 minute until all 4 sides have been cooked – by this time, the heat should have penetrated through and cooked the fish in the centre.

7 Serve with steamed tenderstem broccoli and some boiled crushed new potatoes.

Tip
Instead of making a pesto, you could also use tapenade to flavour the fish.

Homemade chicken nuggets

SERVES 4

4 boneless, skinless chicken
    breasts, cut into strips
50g plain flour
3 eggs, beaten
125g fresh breadcrumbs
3 tbsp vegetable oil
sea salt and freshly ground
    black pepper, to taste

Kids will love helping with these – get them dipping the chicken in the flour, egg and breadcrumbs. For the more adventurous, add lemon zest, sesame seeds or chilli flakes to the breadcrumbs.

1 Season the chicken with salt and black pepper.

2 Tip the flour into a wide shallow bowl, then crack the eggs into a separate bowl and put the breadcrumbs into a third.

3 Starting with the flour, toss the chicken, a few strips at a time, through the flour, then dip into the beaten egg and finally the breadcrumbs, coating the meat totally each time. Use one hand to put them into the flour then the egg, and the other hand to take them out of the eggs and into the breadcrumbs – this way you don't get so sticky! Put the finished nuggets onto a clean plate or tray.

4 Heat a frying pan until medium hot, add 1 tablespoon of the oil and fry the chicken in batches for a couple of minutes on each side until golden and cooked through. Lift out with a slotted spoon and transfer to a plate lined with kitchen paper to drain.

5 Repeat with the remaining oil and chicken until all the nuggets are cooked.

Tip
You could add a little lemon zest, paprika, chilli flakes or ground cumin to the breadcrumbs for extra zing.

Chicken and chickpea curry

SERVES 5

375g whole grain rice
2 tbsp rapeseed oil
2 onions, roughly chopped
2 tbsp medium curry powder
5 boneless, skinless chicken
   thighs, cut into quarters
2 red peppers, deseeded and
   roughly chopped
200g white mushrooms,
   thickly sliced
1 courgette, roughly chopped
400g tin chickpeas, drained
400g tin chopped tomatoes
2 tbsp natural yoghurt
   (optional)
sea salt and freshly ground
   black pepper, to taste
5 tbsp mango chutney, to
   serve
5 naan bread, to serve

This uses chicken thighs to make a really tasty curry with plenty of vegetables and added protein with the chickpeas. If you fancy it a bit hotter, add some chopped chilli and garlic when you have fried the onions.

1 Bring a large pan of water to the boil. Add the rice, stir well, then return to the boil. Simmer for 25–30 minutes until the rice is tender. Drain.

2 While the rice cooks, make the curry. Heat a large frying pan until medium-hot, add the oil, onions and curry powder and cook for 5 minutes until just softened.

3 Turn up the heat, then add the chicken and fry with the onions for a couple of minutes until just golden brown.

4 Add the peppers, mushrooms and courgette and fry for another minute then add the chickpeas and tomatoes and bring to the boil. Reduce the heat and simmer for 15 minutes until the chicken is cooked through and the vegetables are tender.

5 Season to taste with salt and freshly ground black pepper, then stir in the yoghurt, if using, and remove from the heat.

6 Serve the curry with the rice, mango chutney and naan.

Spicy butternut squash and chickpea soup

SERVES 6

1 tbsp olive oil
2 large onions, roughly
    chopped
2 garlic cloves, crushed
1 chilli, deseeded and finely
    chopped
1 tsp ground cumin
1 tsp ground coriander
½ tsp black pepper
140g tomato purée
1 medium butternut squash,
    peeled, deseeded and cut
    into small chunks
1 vegetable stock cube
400g tin chickpeas, drained

Soups don't need to cook for hours – you can make this in 30 minutes.

1 Heat a large frying pan or saucepan until medium hot, add the olive oil and onions and fry for 5 minutes until softened.

2 Add the garlic, chilli, cumin, coriander and black pepper and fry for 1 minute then add the tomato purée and cook for another 2 minutes.

3 Add the butternut squash and coat in all the spices. Crumble in the stock cube and 1.2 litres water, bring to the boil then turn the heat down and simmer for 15 minutes until the squash is soft and the soup slightly reduced.

4 Blend with a stick blender or transfer in batches to a jug blender and blitz until smooth. Return to the heat and stir in the chickpeas.

5 Heat the soup until the chickpeas are hot through, then check the seasoning. Serve straightaway or tip into a sealable container and chill until needed.

Sausage and tomato pasta

SERVES 5

1 tbsp rapeseed oil
6 sausages, cut into chunks
1 large onion, diced
3 garlic cloves, finely chopped
    or grated
1 carrot, peeled and grated
2 tsp dried basil
1 tsp cayenne pepper
1 tsp caster sugar
2 x 400g tins chopped
    tomatoes
375g wholewheat pasta
sea salt and freshly ground
    black pepper, to taste
grated cheese, to serve
garlic bread, to serve

Tip

For a healthier option, have a smaller portion of pasta with a side salad.

Sausages make a great addition to a pasta sauce – ready seasoned and quick to cook, all they need is to be cut into chunks. If you prefer, you can split the skins and remove them before cutting the sausages into chunks.

1 Bring a large saucepan of water to the boil while you start the sauce. Heat a frying pan until hot, add the oil and sausage chunks and fry for 2–3 minutes until browned all over.
2 Turn the heat down a little, add the onion and cook for about 2–3 minutes until just softened.
3 Add the garlic, grated carrot, basil, cayenne pepper and caster sugar and stir well. Fry for 1 minute then add the tinned tomatoes and bring the sauce to the boil. Turn the heat down so that it's just simmering and cook for 10 minutes.
4 By now, the saucepan of water should be boiling. Add a generous pinch of salt and the pasta. Cook the pasta according to the packet instructions until al dente – set a timer on your phone as a reminder! You definitely don't need any oil in the water for cooking the pasta. The oil will stream straight off the pasta as it comes out of the water so it's a waste.
5 When the pasta has cooked, drain it into a colander or sieve then set it back over the saucepan to collect a little of the cooking water.
6 The sauce will now be thickened and the sausages cooked through, so season to taste with salt and black pepper. Tip the drained pasta into the sauce and toss well to coat – if the mixture is a little dry, add the reserved pasta water and stir through really well, then check the seasoning again.
7 Serve with grated cheese and some garlic bread.

Celebrations and Feasts

3

Cheese twists

SERVES 4

320g pack ready-rolled
    all-butter puff pastry
flour, for dusting
1 egg, beaten
2 tsp grain mustard
100g Gruyère, or whatever
    cheese you have to hand,
    grated
sea salt and freshly ground
    black pepper, to taste

There's nothing better than homemade cheese straws – you can use whatever cheese and mustard you fancy. You can even use a thin spread of sandwich pickle or tomato relish for a change – just make sure it's a thin spread otherwise it will ooze out everywhere!

1 Preheat the oven to 200°C/400°F/gas mark 6 and line a baking sheet with silicone paper.

2 Roll out the pastry on a lightly floured worksurface, then brush it first with the beaten egg, then with the grain mustard.

3 Scatter the cheese over the pastry, then season with salt and black pepper. Fold the pastry in half lengthways so that you have a long thin rectangle, then roll it lightly until it is 3mm thick again.

4 Brush with the rest of the egg then season with sea salt and black pepper.

5 Cut the pastry into strips 1.5cm wide, then take the ends of each one at a time in each hand and twist the pastry strip in opposite directions. Place onto the baking sheet.

6 Cook in the oven for 12–15 minutes or until golden brown. Serve hot or cold.

Three ways with bruscetta

These are great snacks, and the broccoli pesto goes really well with spaghetti – make a batch and keep it in the fridge covered in a thin layer of oil.

SERVES 4

1 large baguette, cut into
    1cm thick slices
1 ciabatta loaf, cut into
    1cm thick slices
2 tbsp olive oil
2 garlic cloves, cut in half

For the broccoli pesto
1 head broccoli, chopped
1 garlic clove, chopped
75g pine nuts
50g Parmesan or Grana
    Padano cheese, grated
125ml extra virgin olive oil
sea salt and freshly ground
    black pepper, to taste

For the tomato
4 ripe tomatoes, roughly
    chopped
1 garlic clove, finely chopped
2 tbsp basil leaves, torn
1 tsp extra virgin olive oil
1 tsp red wine vinegar
pinch of sugar (optional)
sea salt and freshly ground
    black pepper, to taste

For the mozzarella
1 ball mozzarella, drained and
    roughly diced
1 tsp chilli oil
sea salt and freshly ground
    black pepper, to taste

The toast

1 Preheat a grill until hot. Brush the bread slices with the olive oil then lay on the grill tray and grill on both sides until just charred around the edges. You may need to do this in batches.
2 Rub the cut side of the garlic halves across the top of the toasted bread, then spread with your preferred topping and serve warm.

Broccoli pesto bruscetta

1 Bring a saucepan of salted water to the boil. Add the broccoli and cook for 3 minutes until just tender. Drain and return to the saucepan then run cold water into it for a minute or two – this will stop the broccoli cooking. (You can do this to any veg that you want to prepare in advance.)
2 Drain the broccoli thoroughly then pat dry with kitchen paper to get rid of any excess water. Place into a food processor or blender along with the garlic, pine nuts and cheese.
3 Blitz to a chunky purée then add the olive oil a little at a time, blending as you go. Add as much or as little oil as you like – depending how thick a pesto you prefer. Season to taste with salt and black pepper and chill until needed.

Tomato bruscetta

1 Tip all the ingredients into a bowl and mix together.
2 Season to taste, adding a pinch of sugar if necessary.
3 Set aside at room temperature until needed – tomatoes are much more flavoursome when they've been allowed to come to room temperature.

Mozzarella bruscetta

1 Toss the mozzarella with the chilli oil then season with salt and black pepper.
2 Set aside to marinate until you are ready to top the bruschetta.

Seafood platter

Make some of the elements of this ahead and you'll have an impressive array of canapés ready to serve at the drop of a hat!

SERVES 6–8

200g smoked salmon
    trimmings
100g cream cheese
75g sour cream or crème
    fraîche
zest and juice of ½ lemon
freshly ground black pepper,
    to taste

To serve
cucumber slices (optional)
small bunch of dill (optional)
24 crostini or mini Melba
    toasts

Smoked salmon pâté

1 Put the salmon, cream cheese, sour cream or crème fraîche, lemon juice and some black pepper into a food processor and blend until you have a rough paste. You don't want it to be totally smooth – you want a little texture.

2 Tip into a serving bowl or a small terrine mould, oiled and lined with a sheet of cling film – this means you will be able to turn it out later. Refrigerate for at least 1 hour or up to 1 week.

3 To serve the pâté, turn upside down onto a plate or board then gently lift the dish off and ease the cling film away from the pâté. You will be left with a smooth-shaped pâté. Garnish with the cucumber slices and dill, if you like, and serve spread on crostini or mini toasts.

SERVES 6–8

½ bulb garlic, unpeeled
150g good-quality
    mayonnaise
250g cooked, peeled jumbo
    king prawns
juice of 1 lemon
small bunch of flat leaf
    parsley, chopped
sea salt and freshly ground
    black pepper, to taste

Roasted garlic mayonnaise and lemon prawns

1 Preheat the oven to 180°C/350°F/gas mark 4.

2 Wrap the garlic in a piece of foil and scrunch up to seal. Roast for 20–30 minutes until the garlic is softened and brown. Set aside to cool.

3 Put the mayonnaise into a bowl and squeeze each clove of garlic out of its papery skin – like squeezing out a toothpaste tube.

4 Mix together with a fork to mash up the garlic. Season with salt and pepper. Cover with cling film and set aside in the fridge for up to 3 days.

5 About 15 minutes before serving, put the prawns into a bowl and squeeze over the lemon juice, tossing to combine. Arrange the lemony prawns in a serving bowl, sprinkle with parsley and season with sea salt and black pepper. Serve the garlic mayonnaise alongside for dipping.

SERVES 6–8

36 canapé blinis
100g smoked salmon
    trimmings
75g sour cream
50g jar lumpfish caviar
½ lemon, for squeezing
freshly ground black pepper,
    to taste (optional)

Smoked salmon and caviar blini canapés

1 Preheat the oven to 200°C/400°F/gas mark 6.

2 Place the blinis on a baking sheet and warm in the oven for about 5 minutes. At the same time, put a serving plate into the oven – you want the blinis to stay warm as long as possible when you serve them.

3 Make sure that the salmon trimmings are cut into manageable pieces ready to top the blinis. Remove the blinis from the oven and transfer to the warmed serving plate.

4 Working quickly, spoon ½ teaspoon of sour cream on each blini. Add a little smoked salmon to the top of 18 of the blinis and a ¼ teaspoon of caviar onto the remaining 18 or mix them together. Squeeze some lemon juice over the salmon blinis and grind over some black pepper, if desired. Serve immediately.

Sticky chicken and veg kebabs

SERVES 4

5 tbsp light olive oil
3 tbsp honey
3 tbsp soy sauce
¼ tsp freshly ground black
    pepper
4 boneless, skinless chicken
    breasts, cut into cubes
2 garlic cloves
2 red peppers, deseeded and
    cut into chunks
1 courgette, cut into chunks
8 cherry tomatoes
1 aubergine, cut into chunks
350g couscous
juice of 1 lemon
sea salt and freshly ground
    black pepper, to taste

You can make these with whatever veg you have to hand, and it works equally well with pork tenderloin.

1 In a large bowl, whisk together 4 tablespoons of the oil, the honey, soy sauce and pepper. Before adding the chicken, reserve a small amount of the marinade to brush onto the kebabs while they are cooking.

2 Place the chicken, garlic and veg in the bowl, toss to coat thoroughly, then cover and marinate in the refrigerator at least 2 hours (the longer the better).

3 When you are ready to cook the kebabs, preheat the oven to 190°C/375°F/gas mark 5.

4 If you are using wooden skewers, run them under the tap to stop them burning during cooking (or soak them in cold water while the chicken marinates). Thread the chicken and vegetables alternately onto the skewers.

5 Place the kebabs into a roasting tin and roast in the oven for about 30 minutes until the chicken is cooked through and the vegetables are tender. Baste with the reserved marinade halfway through cooking.

6 While the chicken cooks, make the couscous. Place the couscous into a large bowl and pour over 350ml of boiling water plus the last tablespoon of olive oil. Stir well, then cover with cling film and set aside for 10 minutes.

7 Run a fork through the couscous to separate the grains, then season with sea salt, black pepper and the lemon juice. Serve with the kebabs.

Puff pastry pizza bites

MAKES 72

A quick, simple canapé for when there are lots of mouths to feed.

For the pizza base
flour, for dusting
2 x 320g packs ready-rolled
    all-butter puff pastry
1 egg, beaten

Tomato and pesto topping
2 tbsp pesto
9 cherry tomatoes, quartered
125g pack mini mozzarella
    balls, drained and
    quartered
pack of fresh basil (optional)
sea salt and freshly ground
    black pepper, to taste

Prosciutto topping
1 onion, very thinly sliced
salt
150ml sour cream
70g prosciutto, roughly
    chopped

1 Preheat the oven to 200°C/400°F/gas mark 6.
2 Lightly flour a work surface and unroll the puff pastry flat. Using a ruler and a pizza wheel, cut it into 72 small, equally sized squares. Transfer the squares to 4 baking trays and brush each with a little of the beaten egg, especially at the edges.
3 For the tomato and pesto bites, using a teaspoon, place a little pesto in the centre of each of 36 squares. Top each with a quarter of a mozzarella ball and a quarter of a tomato. Season with sea salt and black pepper.
4 For the prosciutto bites, place the onion in a bowl and salt generously. (Salting onion draws out the sharpness and begins to soften it.) Using a teaspoon, place a little sour cream in the centre of each of the remaining squares. Rinse the onions under running water and drain well. Place a few slices of onion on each square. Divide the prosciutto among the squares, ensuring that a little fat gets on each piece.
5 Bake both types of pizza for 15 minutes, or until the pastry is puffed and golden brown.
6 The tomato ones can be topped with a basil leaf, if you like, and are best served hot. You can serve the proscuitto pizzas hot or cold.

Bean and veggie fajitas

SERVES 5

10 wholemeal tortilla wraps
1 tbsp oil
1 red onion, finely chopped
1 red pepper, deseeded and
    chopped
2 garlic cloves, finely chopped
1 tsp smoked paprika
1 tsp cayenne pepper
1 tsp ground cumin
400g tin black-eyed beans,
    drained
400g tin red kidney beans,
    drained
½ punnet mushrooms,
    chopped
juice of ½ lemon
2 avocados, stoned and sliced
5 tomatoes, sliced
2 red or green chillies, finely
    sliced
100g natural yoghurt
sea salt and freshly ground
    black pepper, to taste

A healthy, really tasty filling makes these fajitas a great meal for everyone. If you have any leftover bean mix, keep it and use as a filling for jacket potatoes, or alongside rice.

1 Preheat the oven to 200°C/400°F/gas mark 6.
2 Wrap the tortillas in foil ready to pop in the oven a couple of minutes before you're ready to serve up.
3 Heat a frying pan until hot then add the oil, onion, pepper and garlic, turn the heat down and cook for 5–6 minutes until just softened. Cover with a lid to help the vegetables soften and steam.
4 Stir through the smoked paprika, cayenne and ground cumin then add the tinned beans and mix well. Cook over a gentle heat for 7 minutes, stirring occasionally.
5 Add the mushrooms and cook for another 3–4 minutes until tender. At this point, put the tortillas into the oven to heat through.
6 Add the lemon juice and season to taste with sea salt and black pepper.
7 Remove the tortillas from the oven, then serve the bean mix on top of the tortillas, topped with the avocado, tomato, chillies and a dollop of natural yogurt.

Chicken fajitas

SERVES 2 ADULTS,
    3 CHILDREN

10 tortilla wraps
1 large bowl mixed salad –
    lettuce, spinach, grated
    carrot, cucumber, etc
100g mature Cheddar cheese,
    grated
1 tbsp rapeseed oil
4 boneless, skinless chicken
    breasts, cut into 1cm
    thick strips
2 red peppers, deseeded and
    cut into 1cm thick strips
pinch of caster sugar
1 tbsp tomato purée
sea salt and freshly ground
    black pepper, to taste

When you want something quick, fajitas are great and can be assembled at the table – the whole family can get involved.

1 Preheat the oven to 200°C/400°F/gas mark 6.

2 Wrap the tortillas in foil ready to pop in the oven a couple of minutes before you're ready to serve up. The key to this dish is organisation and getting everything ready at the same time, so start by working backwards!

3 Make a large bowl of salad with whatever you want – lettuce, spinach, grated carrot, cucumber, etc. Grate the cheese into a bowl and put both bowls onto the table ready to go.

4 Heat a large frying pan until hot. Add the oil and the chicken and peppers and fry for 3–4 minutes until just coloured. At this point, put the tortillas into the oven to heat through.

5 Add salt, pepper and a pinch of sugar, then stir in the tomato purée to evenly combine. Add a couple of tablespoons of water to the pan and stir through – you want enough to turn the tomato purée into a sauce.

6 Simmer for a couple more minutes until the chicken is cooked through and the peppers are tender. Check the chicken is cooked by slicing one piece in half – it should not be pink in the middle.

7 Tip the chicken and peppers into a serving dish and remove the tortillas from the oven. Serve with the salad and grated cheese, letting everyone dive in and serve themselves.

Tip
Leave out the cheese and add extra salad to your wrap to keep it healthy. If you wish, you could just eat the chicken and peppers with salad and omit the wraps altogether.

Braised shin of beef with creamy mash

SERVES 4–6

6 tbsp rapeseed oil
2 large onions, thinly sliced
4 carrots, peeled and sliced
3 celery sticks, sliced
½ garlic bulb, bashed
3 tbsp plain flour, for dusting
2kg shin of beef, bone in (ask
    your butcher to cut it into
    3cm slices)
500ml ale
300ml beef stock
3–4 sprigs rosemary
sea salt and freshly ground
    black pepper, to taste

For the mashed potato
1kg floury potatoes, such
    as King Edward or Maris
    Piper, peeled and cut into
    4cm cubes
150g salted butter
splash of milk or cream, to
    taste

This beef stew is definitely worth waiting for – rich and delicious and even better when made the day ahead and left to chill overnight. Just return to the hob and heat through very gently until piping hot.

1 Preheat the oven to 160°C/325°F/gas mark 3.

2 Heat a large heavy-bottomed frying pan over a medium heat, add 2 tablespoons of the oil then add the onions, carrots, celery and garlic and fry for a few minutes until they start to turn light golden brown. Transfer to a large casserole dish with a lid.

3 Put the flour onto a plate and season with salt and pepper. Toss the beef in the seasoned flour until coated, then shake off any excess flour. The flour is to thicken the sauce, so you don't want too much flour in the first place or you'll end up with a gloopy sauce.

4 Turn the heat up to high, then add the remaining rapeseed oil to the frying pan. Fry the beef, in batches, for 1 minute on each side until browned all over. Add the beef to the vegetables in the casserole dish.

5 Add a splash of the ale to the frying pan and scrape off any cooked-on pieces of food, then pour it all into the casserole dish. Pour in the remaining ale, the beef stock and rosemary. Bring to a simmer then put it in the oven and cook for 3–4 hours, or until the meat falls easily from the bone. Season to taste with sea salt and black pepper.

6 When there is only 30 minutes left for the beef to cook, put the potatoes into a saucepan and pour in enough water to just cover them. Add a pinch of salt then bring the pan of water to the boil. Simmer for 12–15 minutes until the potatoes are tender, then drain and return to the pan over the heat for a couple of minutes. This will drive off any excess moisture and give a lighter, fluffy mash.

7 Mash until smooth then stir in the butter and milk or cream. Season to taste with salt and pepper and serve with the beef shin.

Five-a-day Moroccan casserole with swiss chard and couscous

SERVES 6

3 tbsp olive oil

5 carrots, peeled and cut into chunks

1 butternut squash, peeled and cut into chunks

3 large courgettes, cut into chunks

2 red peppers, deseeded and cut in 2.5cm chunks

1 yellow pepper, deseeded and cut in 2.5cm chunks

2 red onions, cut into wedges

4 garlic cloves, thinly sliced

1 tsp ground coriander

2 tsp smoked paprika

2 tsp ground cinnamon

1 tsp ground cumin

2 x 400g tins chopped tomatoes

1 tbsp harissa paste

2 tbsp clear honey

small bunch of coriander, finely chopped

200g dried apricots, halved

2 x 400g tins chickpeas, drained and rinsed

350g couscous

100g sultanas

zest and juice of 1½ lemons

1 tsp rapeseed oil

large handful of rainbow chard, stalks finely diced and leaves coarsely cut

2 garlic cloves, finely sliced

sea salt and freshly ground black pepper, to taste

Easy to prepare and extremely good for you, this is a delicious spicy and vegetable-filled casserole.

1 Preheat the oven to 190°C/375°F/gas mark 5.

2 Heat a large frying pan until hot, then add 1 tablespoon of the olive oil. Add half the carrots, squash, courgettes and peppers and fry for 3–4 minutes until just coloured. Remove and set aside, then repeat with another tablespoon of oil and the remaining vegetables. Season well with salt and pepper.

3 Heat a large casserole dish until hot, then add the last tablespoon of oil and the onions and fry for 3–5 minutes, until softened. Add the garlic, ground coriander, smoked paprika, cinnamon and cumin, mix well and fry for 1–2 minutes.

4 Add the chopped tomatoes, harissa paste, honey, fresh coriander, apricots and chickpeas and stir together. Add the sautéed vegetables to the dish and stir well. Cover and place the casserole in the oven to bake for 20 minutes.

5 Remove the casserole from the oven and carefully add 200ml cold water, stir well then return to the oven to cook for 10 minutes. The vegetables should now be tender and the sauce thickened. Season to taste with salt and black pepper.

6 While the casserole cooks, prepare the couscous and chard. Place the couscous and sultanas into a large bowl and pour over 350ml of boiling water plus the zest and juice of 1 lemon. Stir well, then cover with cling film and leave for 10 minutes.

7 Meanwhile, heat a medium frying pan until medium hot, add the rapeseed oil, garlic and chard stalks and cook for a few minutes until the leaves have wilted.

8 Stir in the remaining lemon zest and juice and season to taste with salt and black pepper.

9 Run a fork through the couscous to separate the grains, then season with sea salt and black pepper. Serve with the chard and the casserole.

Roast chicken thighs with asparagus and courgette

SERVES 4

8 chicken thighs, skin on
4 tsp rapeseed oil
1 tsp dried thyme or oregano
2 courgettes, topped and
    tailed and cut into batons
12 asparagus stems, woody
    bases removed
sea salt and freshly ground
    black pepper, to taste

Roasted chicken thighs are like a mini roast chicken – you get crispy skin and succulent meat but in a fraction of the time.

1 Preheat the oven to 200°C/400°F/gas mark 6.
2 Pat the chicken dry with kitchen paper then score the skin with a knife, cutting just through into the flesh. Drizzle 2 teaspoons of the oil over the chicken then season with salt, pepper and the thyme or oregano. Rub into the chicken well, making sure they are fully coated, then place in a roasting tin and transfer to the oven to cook for 10 minutes.
3 Meanwhile, prepare the vegetables. Toss them in the remaining oil and season with salt and black pepper.
4 After 10 minutes, add the courgettes and asparagus to the tin with the chicken and roast for another 10–15 minutes until the chicken is cooked through and the vegetables are tender. To test if the chicken is cooked, insert a knife into the fattest part of the chicken and remove. If the knife is hot and the juices run clear, the chicken is cooked – if not, return to the oven for another 5 minutes, but remove the vegetables first as you don't want them overcooked.
5 Serve the chicken with tomato and basil pasta, mash or rice.

Hasselback potatoes with bacon

SERVES 4

1kg small baby potatoes
300g bacon rashers, each cut
    into 3 strips
freshly ground black pepper

These look really impressive and you can do them with baby or large potatoes – just cook them for longer for the larger ones.

1 Preheat the oven to 200°C/400°F/gas mark 6.
2 Cut narrow slices into the potatoes, but not all the way down to the base – place the potato you are cutting right next to a teaspoon handle so that when you are cutting the knife can't go all the way down to the chopping board. Make the slices a little narrower than a pound coin.
3 Wrap each potato in half a rasher of bacon and place seam down onto a baking tray, then season with black pepper.
4 Bake for 30–40 minutes, or until the potatoes are cooked through and the bacon is crispy.

Roast chicken dinner with trimmings

SERVES 4–6

1 lemon
6 garlic cloves, peeled
3 onions, cut into wedges
3 carrots, peeled and cut into
    large chunks
3 red peppers, deseeded and
    cut into quarters
4 tsp olive oil
6 sprigs thyme
1 medium chicken
5 heaped tsp gravy granules
sea salt and freshly ground
    black pepper, to taste

1 Preheat the oven to 200°C/400°F/gas mark 6.

2 Prick the lemon several times with a fork or knife then pop it in a microwave on High for 40 seconds. This quick blast will help release all the juices – make sure it's no more than 40 seconds, though, as you don't want to burn the lemon!

3 While the lemon is in the microwave, place the garlic, onions, carrots and peppers into a deep-sided roasting tray with 2 teaspoons of the oil and half the thyme and toss well to coat. Season with salt and black pepper.

4 Place the chicken on top of the vegetables, then cut the lemon in half and place both halves inside the cavity of the chicken with the remaining thyme. Drizzle 2 more teaspoons of the oil over the chicken and rub it into the skin, then season with some sea salt and black pepper.

5 Put the tray in the oven and roast for 1½ hours. After 45 minutes, remove the tray from the oven and baste the chicken by spooning any juices from the bottom of the tray over the bird. Pour in 100ml of water, wriggling the tray around to evenly distribute it, then spoon the juices over the chicken again.

6 If you are roasting potatoes with the chicken (see opposite page), add them now for the last 45 minutes of its cooking time, turning the potatoes over after 30 minutes.

7 Check that the chicken is cooked by inserting a knife or skewer into the fattest part of the thigh. If the juices run clear, the chicken is cooked through. If any blood comes out, return it to the oven for another 10 minutes then check again.

8 Remove the chicken from the tray, lift it onto a platter and cover with foil. Using a slotted spoon, transfer the vegetables from the tray to a serving bowl and cover with foil. Check the potatoes are tender and browned, then turn the oven down to low to keep them hot. If they are not tender, leave the oven at the same temperature so they can cook a little longer while you make the gravy.

9 Put the roasting tray of cooking juices onto the hob over a medium heat and bring the liquid to the boil, scraping up any juicy bits stuck on the bottom. Add 300ml of water to the tray and return to the boil, stirring all the time. While the liquid comes to the boil, tip the gravy granules into a heatproof jug or bowl and place a sieve over the top. Pour the boiling juices from the tray through the sieve onto the granules, then remove the sieve and whisk really well until the granules have dissolved and the gravy is smooth and thickened.

10 Tip any juices that have collected underneath the chicken while resting on the platter into the gravy and stir them through. Season the gravy to taste with salt and black pepper.

11 Remove the potatoes from the oven and transfer to a serving bowl. Carve the legs from the chicken, then cut them in half through the joint between the drumstick and thigh. Carve away the breasts and cut them into slices. Turn the carcass over and remove the piece of meat on either side of the backbone – this is normally the chef's treat, a lovely juicy, tasty piece of chicken! Serve the chicken with the roast potatoes, roasted vegetables and a good glug of gravy.

Roast potatoes

SERVES 4–6

50g lard, dripping or
    vegetable oil
10 King Edward or Maris
    Piper potatoes, peeled and
    cut into 2 or 3
sea salt and freshly ground
    black pepper, to taste

There's nothing nicer than a crunchy yet fluffy roast potato – here's a foolproof way of how to do it, with a proper Yorkshire pudding to go alongside on the next page if you fancy it.

1 Preheat the oven to 200°C/400°F/gas mark 6. Put the lard, dripping or vegetable oil into a deep roasting tin and place in the oven to heat.

2 Put the potatoes into a large saucepan, add enough cold water to just cover and a pinch of salt and bring to the boil. Reduce the heat and simmer for 3–4 minutes until just cooked around the edges but not cooked through.

3 Drain into a colander and shake around a little to roughen up the edges – you want these to be broken up slightly so that they go lovely and crunchy when you roast them.

4 Season with salt and black pepper then tip into the tin in the oven, taking care not to splash the oil. Turn them around in the hot fat so that they are coated, then slide back into the oven. Leave them to roast for 25–30 minutes until starting to turn golden brown, then turn them around in the tray and roast for another 20 minutes until golden brown and crispy. Serve straightaway.

SERVES 4–6

small mug plain flour
small mug eggs
small mug semi-skimmed milk
50g lard, dripping or
    vegetable oil
sea salt and freshly ground
    black pepper, to taste

Tip
These can be made in
advance then frozen or
chilled and reheated on a
baking tray in the oven for
5 minutes.

Yorkshire pudding

1 Take a small mug and fill it with the flour, then tip into a large bowl and make a well in the centre.

2 Fill the mug with as many eggs as it takes, then tip that onto the flour. Refill the mug with milk and set to one side.

3 Whisk the eggs into the flour, gradually pulling the flour in from the sides and adding a little of the milk as you go.

4 Keep mixing, pulling the flour in and adding the milk until you have a smooth, thick batter. Season with salt and black pepper then cover and refrigerate for at least 4 hours, preferably overnight.

5 Preheat the oven to 220°C/425°F/gas mark 7. Divide the dripping or lard among a 12-hole muffin tin and place in the oven for 10 minutes until smoking hot.

6 Pull out the oven rack that the tin is on as far as possible, then, using a jug, pour the batter into the tin. You only want it to be about two-thirds full.

7 Slide the tin back into the oven and bake for 20 minutes without opening the door – you want a really high constant heat to help the puddings rise.

8 Open the door a crack to let out any steam, then turn the oven down to 180°C/350°F/gas mark 4. Continue to cook for another 15 minutes until crispy and golden brown.

Parmesan roast carrots and parsnips

SERVES 6–8

7–8 carrots, peeled and
    trimmed
7–8 parsnips, peeled and
    trimmed
3 tbsp olive oil
30g Parmesan cheese, grated
sea salt and freshly ground
    black pepper, to taste

Parboiling these carrots and parsnips before roasting means they take less time in the oven.

1 Preheat the oven to 200°C/400°F/gas mark 6.
2 Cut the carrots and parsnips in half lengthways and cut any particularly large pieces in half again. Bring a large saucepan of water to the boil and add the vegetables. Boil for 3 minutes, or until the vegetables are just beginning to soften (you want them to keep their shape while roasting).
3 Drain well and divide between 2 roasting tins (if the tin is crowded the vegetables won't crisp up well). Add the oil and mix to coat the vegetables. Season with salt and pepper and top with the grated Parmesan.
4 Roast for 25 minutes or until the carrots and parsnips are golden brown at the edges.

Tips
To make ahead, simply remove the vegetables from the oven 5 minutes before the end of the cooking time. Leave to cool, then transfer to the freezer. To reheat, tip the frozen vegetables into a roasting tin and roast for 10–15 minutes, or until piping hot. Make the process easier by using disposable foil roasting tins, which can also be frozen.

Make-ahead gravy

SERVES 4

3 carrots, peeled and roughly
    chopped
1 red onion, cut into wedges
5 chicken wings
1 tbsp light olive oil or
    vegetable oil
1 large glass white wine
    (optional)
1–2 tbsp cornflour, depending
    on how thick you like your
    gravy
2 litres chicken or turkey
    stock
sea salt and freshly ground
    black pepper, to taste

A good gravy is a thing of joy – make a large batch, divide it into
small portions and freeze so you always have some to hand.

1 Preheat the oven to 200°C/400°F/gas mark 6.

2 Coat the carrots, onion and chicken wings in the oil in a roasting
tin. Place the tin into the oven and roast for 45 minutes until the
chicken is golden brown and the vegetables are soft.

3 Put the roasting tin on the hob over a medium heat. Add the
white wine, if using, or pour in a glass of water. Deglaze the tin and
scrape off any caramelised bits on the bottom of the tin. Remove
from the heat.

4 Use a slotted spoon to transfer the vegetables and chicken to a
large saucepan, and stir in the cornflour until combined. Add the
liquid from the roasting tin and the stock, bring to the boil and
simmer for 15–20 minutes. As it bubbles away, use a fork to break
up the chicken and vegetables as much as you can.

5 Strain the gravy through a fine sieve into a freezeable container,
pushing through as much of the chicken and vegetables as you
can. Season to taste with salt and pepper.

6 Allow the gravy to cool completely, then cover with a lid and
transfer to the freezer. (The gravy will keep in the freezer for up to
3 months.) Defrost the gravy in the fridge overnight before using.

7 Reheat in the microwave for 4 minutes on high or, if you have
time, add it to the roasting tin when you have removed your roast
chicken or turkey to rest. Heat the gravy gently in the tin, stirring it
and scraping up any bits from the bottom of the tin to thoroughly
incorporate all the flavours from the roast. Once hot, pour into a
serving jug.

Make-ahead red cabbage

SERVES 6–8

knob of butter
2 tbsp olive oil
1 onion, finely sliced or
    chopped
1 tsp ground cinnamon
½ tsp ground nutmeg
600g red cabbage, shredded
    finely using a food
    processor (white core
    discarded)
3 tbsp soft brown sugar
3 eating apples, peeled, cored
    and diced
150ml red wine vinegar
2 tsp redcurrant or cranberry
    sauce
sea salt and freshly ground
    black pepper, to taste

A year round staple for a roast dinner, this red cabbage can be made ahead of time and frozen in batches to be easily defrosted when needed.

1 Heat a large saucepan until medium hot, add the butter, oil and onion and sweat gently for 5–8 minutes until the onion is softened. Stir in the spices then add the cabbage and fry for 3–4 minutes, stirring occasionally, until glossy.

2 Stir in the sugar, apples and red wine vinegar. Bring to the boil then turn the heat down, cover with a lid and let it cook gently for 30 minutes.

3 Stir in the redcurrant or cranberry sauce and cook for a further 10 minutes. By now the cabbage should be soft and glossy. Season to taste with salt and black pepper.

Tips
- The cabbage should be cooked for 15–20 minutes more if it isn't finely shredded.
- This dish freezes well. Let the cooked cabbage cool completely, then transfer to a freezerproof container (it will keep in the freezer for 3 months). Defrost in the microwave or overnight in the fridge, then reheat in a microwave or in a saucepan on the hob.

Shredded sprouts with chestnuts and bacon

SERVES 4–6

2 tbsp olive oil
200g bacon lardons or sliced
    streaky bacon
180g pack ready-to-eat
    chestnuts, roughly
    chopped
500g Brussels sprouts
juice of 1 lemon
sea salt and freshly ground
    black pepper

For the breadcrumbs (optional)
100g fresh breadcrumbs
large knob of butter or 2 tbsp
    olive oil
zest of 1 lemon

For those that are dubious about sprouts, shred them up and fry them with some bacon and tinned cooked chestnuts – a delicious alternative to soggy sprouts!

1 Heat a frying pan until hot, add 1 tablespoon of the olive oil and the bacon and fry until very crisp and the fat has rendered off.
2 Remove from the heat and stir in the chestnuts. Transfer to a bowl or plastic tub, taking care to include as much of the oil from the pan as possible. Cool, then store in the fridge for up to 3 days.
3 Trim the sprouts to remove any blemished leaves or stalks. Set up a food processor with the shredder attachment and shred the sprouts. Transfer to a food bag, seal and store in the fridge for up to 24 hours.
4 When ready to cook, add the remaining olive oil to a large frying pan (if your pan isn't big enough, cook the sprouts in 2 batches). Add the bacon, chestnuts and any fat and fry for 1–2 minutes. Tip in the sprouts and fry for 3–5 minutes (depending on how crunchy you like your veg), stirring all the time. Add the lemon juice and season with salt and pepper.
5 If making the breadcrumbs, fry them in butter or oil with the lemon zest until golden brown and crisp (about 3 minutes). Stir into the sprouts and serve immediately.

4

Love your Leftovers

Sunday lunch leftovers

It's easy to make too much for a Sunday lunch, so here are three simple recipes to make tasty meals from leftovers.

SERVES 6

Hot coronation turkey

6 cooked Yorkshire pudding
    cases
15g butter
1 onion, finely chopped
1 tbsp curry powder
2 tsp tomato purée
200g mango chutney
450g cooked turkey or
    chicken, diced
450g Greek-style yoghurt
sea salt and freshly ground
    black pepper, to taste

Tip
You don't want to boil the sauce or it will split.

You can use turkey or chicken for this twist on a classic dish, just remember not to boil it once the yoghurt goes in.

1 Preheat the oven to 210°C/410°F/gas mark 7. Place the Yorkshire puddings onto a baking tray ready to go into the oven later.

2 Heat a frying pan until medium hot, then add the butter and onion and cook for 5 minutes until the onion is just softened.

3 Add the curry powder and tomato purée, mix well and cook for a further minute, then add the chutney and cook for another couple of minutes.

4 Add the turkey or chicken, stir well and cook for 5 minutes until the meat is hot right through. At this point, put the Yorkshire puddings into the oven to heat – they will only take a few minutes.

5 Stir the yoghurt into the curry and heat through until just simmering, then season to taste with salt and black pepper.

6 Serve the coronation turkey or chicken spooned into the Yorkshire pudding cases.

Leftover vegetable soup

300g (approx) leftover roast
    potatoes, roughly chopped
400g (approx) cooked
    vegetables, roughly
    chopped
1–1½ litres stock
sea salt and freshly ground
    black pepper, to taste
grated cheese, to serve

Leftover veg are put to good use in a soup here – cook just long
enough for them to be hot all the way through before blending.

1 Put the potatoes and vegetables in a pan that will hold them
snugly in the bottom and about halfway up the side.
2 Cover the veg with stock by about 2cm – go easy, you can always
add more liquid later to adjust the consistency of the soup.
3 Bring to the boil, then reduce the heat and cook for about
10 minutes or until thoroughly heated through.
4 Liquidise the soup with a hand-held electric blender to your
preferred texture – add a little more stock if it needs it. Taste the
soup and season – this is one soup that needs plenty of pepper.
5 Serve in mugs or bowls with grated cheese scattered over.

MAKES 12

Leftover vegetable scones

375g plain flour, plus extra for
    dusting
1 tsp sea salt
1 tbsp baking powder
50g cooked leftover
    vegetables, roughly
    chopped
200g cooked mashed swede
250ml milk
25g grated cheese

You would never believe that leftover mashed swede could be
turned into delicious scones, but be prepared to be amazed!

1 Preheat the oven to 220°C/425°F/gas mark 7. Line a baking
tray with baking parchment.
2 Put the flour, salt, baking powder and leftover chopped
vegetables into a large bowl and mix together.
3 Mix the swede and milk together in a separate bowl then
gradually add this to the flour and vegetable mixture, a little at
a time, until you have a stiff dough. It needs to be firm enough
to pat out but not so sticky that it sticks to your hands.
4 Tip out the dough onto a lightly floured surface then flatten
it gently with the palm of your hand to about 2cm thick. Dust a
6.5–7cm round cutter with flour and use it to stamp out
about 12 rounds from the dough.
5 Place the rounds onto the baking tray then sprinkle them with a
little cheese and bake for 15 minutes until golden. Serve warm.

Turkey pâté

SERVES 4–6

75g butter
1 large onion, chopped
400g cold cooked turkey or
    chicken, roughly chopped
60ml single cream
60ml dry sherry
2 tbsp flat leaf parsley,
    roughly chopped
sea salt and freshly ground
    black pepper, to taste

To serve
crackers and crispbreads
cranberry relish

A super-quick way to make pate, perfect for using up leftover turkey or chicken

1 Heat a frying pan until medium hot, add the butter and onion, stir well then cover and cook gently for 10 minutes until the onion is transparent and soft.
2 Remove from the heat and tip into a food processor with the turkey or chicken meat. Blitz to a chunky purée then add the cream and sherry and blitz once more until nearly smooth.
3 Season to taste with salt and black pepper then add the parsley and blitz once more.
4 Spoon the pâté into a large serving dish or individual ramekins. Cover with cling film and chill in the fridge for at least 3 hours.
5 Serve with crackers and crispbreads and some cranberry relish.

Spicy falafel with couscous and chilli yoghurt dip

SERVES 4

400g tin red kidney beans,
    drained and rinsed
400g tin chickpeas, drained
    and rinsed
1 tsp garlic paste
1 tsp ground cumin
1 tsp ground coriander
1 tsp smoked paprika
1 tsp lemon juice
1 egg
small bunch of coriander,
    roughly chopped
2–3 tbsp olive oil
sea salt and freshly ground
    black pepper, to taste

For the couscous
250g couscous
1 tsp lemon juice
1 tbsp olive oil
400g tin green beans, drained
    and chopped
195g tin sweetcorn, drained
small jar roasted red peppers,
    drained and roughly
    chopped
small bunch of parsley,
    roughly chopped
sea salt and freshly ground
    black pepper, to taste

For the yoghurt dip
2 tbsp chilli sauce
200g Greek or natural yoghurt
sea salt and freshly ground
    black pepper, to taste

Falafel are great as a snack in a pitta bread or as a full meal with couscous or salad – here they're made with kidney beans for some extra added protein.

1 Preheat the oven to 210°C/410°C/gas mark 7. Line a baking sheet with baking parchment.

2 Put all the ingredients for the falafel except the olive oil into a food processor and blitz to a rough purée. Stop and scrape the sides down, then repeat until you have a slightly grainy mixture. Stopping and scraping the sides halfway through means you get a nice even purée, rather than a coarse/fine mixed one.

3 Divide the mixture in half, then half again and then into 4 – you will have 16 spoonfuls. Run your hands under cold water then gently form the spoonfuls into balls and set onto the lined sheet.

4 Heat a frying pan until hot, add the olive oil and falafel and fry on each side until golden brown. Lift out of the pan onto a baking tray and place in the oven to bake for 15 minutes until hot through and crunchy on the outside.

5 While the falafel bake, make the couscous and dip. Place the couscous into a large bowl and pour over 250ml of boiling water plus the lemon juice and olive oil. Stir well, then cover with cling film and leave for 10 minutes.

6 Run a fork through the couscous to separate the grains, then stir in all the vegetables and herbs. Season with salt and black pepper then stir through once more.

7 Finally, make the yoghurt dip. Stir the chilli sauce into the yoghurt and season to taste.

8 Serve the falafel with the couscous and chilli yoghurt.

Baked eggs

SERVES 5

1 tbsp oil
2 onions, chopped
1 chilli, finely chopped
2 garlic cloves, finely chopped
   or grated
1 tsp caster sugar
2 tsp smoked paprika
2 tsp dried basil
2 x 400g tins chopped
   tomatoes
75g sundried tomatoes,
   roughly chopped
400g tin butter beans,
   drained
5 eggs
200g feta, roughly chopped
sea salt and freshly ground
   black pepper, to taste
part-baked baguettes, to serve

Eggs go with many things, and tomatoes and spices are a great combination here with the beans and eggs – a fairly substantial vegetarian lunch.

1 Preheat the oven to 200°C/400°F/gas mark 6.
2 Heat a large ovenproof frying pan until hot, add the oil, onions, chilli and garlic and cook for a few minutes until just softened.
3 Add the caster sugar, paprika and basil, stir through then add both the tinned and sundried tomatoes and the butter beans. Bring to the boil, then turn the heat down to a simmer and cook for about 8–10 minutes until just thickened – if it simmers too rapidly it might dry out, if so you will need to add a splash of water.
4 Season with salt and black pepper and stir well.
5 Make 5 small indents in the mixture then crack an egg into each well.
6 Scatter the feta over the top of the whole dish and place in the oven for 8–12 minutes – if you like a runny egg, just cook for 8 minutes, otherwise 12 minutes for a firm egg. Place the baguettes in the oven at the same time to bake.
7 Divide among 5 bowls, making sure there is an egg in each, and serve with the baguettes.

Tips
- You can adapt this recipe by using any combination of your favourite ingredients – chorizo and halloumi, garlic mushrooms and Parmesan, chilli and olives, etc. – whatever you have in your cupboards.
- If you don't have an ovenproof pan, make the sauce in a pan then tip it into a ceramic baking dish or casserole before adding the eggs and baking.

Leftover ham croquettes

SERVES 4

15g butter
½ onion, finely chopped
450g leftover mashed
    potatoes
75g ham, roughly chopped
2 tbsp cooked sweetcorn
2 tbsp cooked peas
2 cooked carrots, roughly
    chopped
2 tbsp flat leaf parsley,
    roughly chopped
50g plain flour
1 egg, beaten
75g fresh breadcrumbs (from
    leftover bread)
4 tbsp vegetable oil
sea salt and freshly ground
    black pepper, to taste
green salad, to serve

Never throw away your leftover mashed potatoes – turn them into crispy yet soft croquettes with a handful of ham and some leftover cooked vegetables.

1 Heat a small frying pan until medium-hot then add the butter and onion and fry for 5 minutes until the onion is just coloured and softened. Remove from the heat and tip the onion into a large bowl to cool.

2 When the onion is cool, add the leftover mashed potato and mix well to combine.

3 Add the ham, sweetcorn, peas, carrots and parsley and mix really well until combined. Season to taste – the mixture needs to be quite firm and not too floppy.

4 Divide the mixture in half, then half again and finally into 4 so that you have 16 spoonfuls. Gently roll each one into a small sausage shape and set them on a plate or baking tray.

5 Tip the flour into a wide shallow bowl, then crack the egg into a separate bowl and the breadcrumbs into a third.

6 Starting with the flour, roll the potato sausages a few at a time through the flour, then dip into the beaten egg and finally the breadcrumbs, coating them totally each time. Put the finished croquettes onto a clean plate or baking tray. Use one hand to put them in the flour, then egg and the other hand to take them out of the egg and into the breadcrumbs – this way you don't get your hands so sticky!

7 Place the croquettes in the fridge for 30 minutes to firm up before cooking.

8 When you are ready to cook, preheat the oven to 210°C/410°F/gas mark 7.

9 Heat a frying pan until hot, add 1 tablespoon of the vegetable oil and heat it through, then add some of the croquettes and fry on each side until golden brown. Repeat with the rest of the oil and the croquettes. Transfer the cooked croquettes to a clean baking tray and when they have all been cooked, place in the oven to heat through for 5 minutes.

10 Serve with a green salad.

Leftover chicken stir-fry with sesame noodles

SERVES 4

4 nests egg noodles
1 tsp toasted sesame oil
1 tbsp vegetable oil
1 onion, finely sliced
1 garlic clove, finely chopped
1 red chilli, deseeded and
    finely chopped
5cm piece of fresh root
    ginger, peeled and finely
    chopped
400g cooked chicken, cut
    into strips
75g cooked carrots, sliced
75g cooked green beans,
    halved
2 tbsp soy sauce
zest and juice of 1 orange
1 tbsp sesame seeds

Spice up leftover roast chicken and veg with a quick stir-fry – make it as spicy as you like.

1 Bring a saucepan of water to the boil, add the noodles and cook according to the packet instructions. Drain and toss with the toasted sesame oil.
2 Meanwhile, heat a wok until hot, add the vegetable oil and onion and stir-fry for 2 minutes until the onion is just softening.
3 Add the garlic, chilli and ginger and fry for 1 minute, then add the cooked chicken, carrots and green beans and cook until hot through, stir-frying all the time – it should take 2–3 minutes.
4 Add the soy sauce and orange zest and juice and heat through.
5 Add the sesame noodles to the chicken and heat through, then serve immediately with the sesame seeds sprinkled over the top.

Tip
You can use whatever meat and vegetables you have leftover, just remember to make sure that everything is heated through until piping hot.

Vegetable crisps

SERVES 4

extra-virgin olive oil spray
1 carrot
1 sweet potato
1 courgette
1–2 tsp nutritional yeast, to
    taste

A really low-fat alternative to crisps – just cut them as thinly as possible to get a really good crisp.

1 Preheat the oven to 200°C/400°F/gas mark 6.

2 Line 2 baking trays with foil then spray with the olive oil spray.

3 Peel the carrot and discard the outer layer, then continue peeling the carrot until there is nothing left – you will have a big pile of carrot shavings.

4 Repeat with the sweet potato and courgette – don't discard the outer layer of the courgette, though. Cut the sweet potato in half if it's too big for your peeler to get one slice across it.

5 Remove any excess moisture from the shavings by pressing them between sheets of kitchen paper.

6 Lay the shavings onto the foiled baking trays, making sure they are not overlapping, then spray them with the oil.

7 Bake in the oven for 10 minutes until beginning to crisp then shuffle them around a little – turning them over if needed. Return to the oven for another 5 minutes, then check as they will catch quite quickly! If they are not quite crisp, return to the oven for a few more minutes, but remember they will crisp up as they cool.

8 Remove from the oven and leave to cool and crisp up.

9 Sprinkle with the nutritional yeast to taste and serve.

Veggie tempura with chilli dip

oil, for deep-frying
150g mayonnaise
2 tbsp chilli sauce
50g plain flour
50g cornflour
pinch of sea salt, plus extra
    to serve
150–200ml sparkling water
1 courgette, cut into 5mm
    thick slices
1 red pepper, deseeded and
    cut into slices
1 yellow pepper, deseeded
    and cut into slices
1 red onion, cut into 1cm
    thick wedges with the root
    left on
12 baby sweetcorn
½ jar sliced artichoke hearts,
    drained

This is a great quick little starter or snack – a light crisp batter that you can use with any vegetables that you would normally stir-fry or even prawns.

1 Heat a deep-fat fryer to 190°C/375°F, or heat the oil for deep-frying in a deep, heavy-based frying pan until a breadcrumb sizzles and turns brown when dropped in. The oil should only come halfway up the side of the deep-fat fryer or pan. (CAUTION: Hot oil can be dangerous. Do not leave unattended.)

2 Whisk the mayonnaise and chilli sauce together in a small bowl.

3 Tip both the flours into a large bowl with the salt and mix together, then whisk in enough sparkling water to make a double-cream-like consistency.

4 Dip the vegetables into the batter a few at a time then transfer them straight into the hot deep-fat fryer and fry for 2–3 minutes – the batter should be crispy and the vegetables just tender. Lift out onto kitchen paper to drain, then repeat with the remaining vegetables and batter.

5 Place the cooked vegetables onto a serving platter then season with salt and serve the dip alongside.

5

Treats and Snacks

Gluten-free lemon shortbread with lemon and blueberry fool

SERVES 4, PLUS EXTRA
SHORTBREAD

For shortbread
200g butter, softened, plus
extra for greasing
125g caster sugar, plus extra
for dusting
zest of 1 lemon
1 tbsp vanilla extract
225g gluten-free plain flour
100g rice flour

For lemon fool
400g 0%-fat Greek yoghurt
zest of 1 lemon
4 tbsp maple syrup
160g frozen blueberries

Note
If using a multi-purpose flour
like Glutafin white mix flour,
decrease the sugar in the
shortbread to 75g as the mix
has sugar in it.

These are really easy to make and taste delicious – everyone will love them, gluten free or not!

1 Preheat the oven to 180°C/350°F/gas mark 4. Grease and line the base of a 23 x 30cm traybake tin with baking parchment.

2 Beat the butter and sugar together in a large bowl until soft. Add the lemon zest and vanilla extract and beat in.

3 Add both the flours and mix together until the mixture starts to form a dough – do not pull it together too much at this stage.

4 Press the dough into the tin – it will be a little crumbly, but just press down gently into the corners and all along so that you have an even layer of shortbread. When it is nice and even, prick it all over with a fork and sprinkle a little caster sugar on top.

5 Bake in the oven for 25–30 minutes until pale golden brown. Remove and leave to cool for 5 minutes before cutting into 18 fingers in the tin. Leave to cool totally before serving.

6 While the shortbread cools, make the fool. Put the yoghurt into a medium bowl with the lemon zest and half the maple syrup and mix until combined.

7 Place spoonfuls of the lemon yoghurt into 4 serving glasses or bowls, then top with a spoonful of blueberries and a drizzle of maple syrup. Repeat the layers until everything is used up.

8 Either serve the fool straightaway with the lemon shortbread or cover and place in the fridge until ready to serve. It's nice to serve this when the blueberries are still frozen as you get a satisfying pop of fruit.

Tips
- You can use coconut flour instead of the gluten-free flour – any number of different flours are available. Experiment with different flours and find your favourite.
- You can layer up any frozen fruit with the yoghurt, or use soft fruit if it is in season.

Banana and peanut butter ice cream

SERVES 4

4 ripe bananas, chopped into
    3cm chunks then frozen
2 tbsp almond milk
1 tbsp peanut butter
1 tsp ground cinnamon, plus
    extra (optional)
1 tbsp dark chocolate, grated,
    to serve
1 tbsp flaked almonds, to
    serve

An instant ice cream that doesn't need churning, this is a great way to use up over ripe bananas. In fact, the sweeter the banana, the better the ice cream!

1 Tip the frozen bananas and almond milk into a blender. Blitz together to a smooth and creamy consistency. Add the peanut butter and cinnamon and blitz again until combined. Taste and add more cinnamon, if you like.

2 Transfer to a freezerproof container and freeze for 1 hour.

3 Take out of the freezer and serve with grated chocolate and flaked almonds sprinkled over.

Breakfast smoothie

SERVES 2

500ml semi-skimmed milk
2 tbsp mixed frozen fruits
    (choose your favourites)
2 tbsp blanched almonds
2 tbsp rolled oats
1 tsp runny honey (optional)

A perfect start to the day – fruit, carbohydrate, calcium and protein all in one glassful. Use whichever fruit you have to hand.

Put all the ingredients into a blender and blitz until smooth. Serve straightaway or tip into a sealed container and chill until needed.

Chocolate cookies

MAKES 16

75g butter, softened
80g soft light brown sugar
1 tsp vanilla extract
1 medium egg
125g self-raising flour
50g plain chocolate chips
50g milk chocolate chips

A classic chocolate cookie that will disappear very quickly! You can ring the changes and substitute fruit and/or nuts for the chocolate – just keep the quantity the same.

1 Preheat the oven to 190°C/375°F/gas mark 5. Line a baking tray with baking parchment.
2 Beat the butter and sugar together until really soft and fluffy. Add the vanilla extract and egg and beat once more until the egg has disappeared into the mixture.
3 Fold in the flour and all the chocolate chips – you will have a soft, sticky dough.
4 Divide the dough in half, then half again, then finally into 4 – you will have 16 small balls of dough. Place them all onto the baking tray, making sure there's a gap between each of them.
5 Bake in the oven for 8–10 minutes until just light golden brown and still slightly gooey in the middle.
6 Leave to cool on the baking tray for at least 5 minutes, then transfer to a wire rack to cool, or eat straightaway!

Eggless beetroot and chocolate cake

SERVES 8

100ml rapeseed oil, plus
    extra for greasing
200g vacuum packed, natural
    cooked beetroot, drained
    and roughly chopped
200g dark soft brown sugar
200g 0%-fat natural yoghurt
2 tsp vanilla extract
¼ tsp sea salt
200g self-raising flour
1 tbsp baking powder
50g cocoa powder

This is a dark, rich, delicious cake with a slight saintliness about it – good enough to serve as a dessert with a spoonful of crème fraîche and handful of raspberries.

1 Preheat the oven to 180°C/350°F/gas mark 4. Grease and line the base of a 20cm deep-sided, loose-bottomed cake tin.

2 Put the beetroot, oil and sugar into a blender and blitz to a smooth purée.

3 Tip the yoghurt, vanilla extract and salt into a large bowl and whisk together, then stir in the beetroot mixture and mix really well.

4 Sift the flour, baking powder and cocoa powder onto the mixture and fold in to make a smooth batter.

5 Pour into the prepared tin and bake the cake in the oven for 35–40 minutes until risen and set – a skewer inserted into the centre of the cake should come out clean – if not, return to the oven for another 5 minutes and test again.

6 Remove and cool in the tin before turning out – it will collapse down slightly, but don't fear, that's normal!

7 Serve with a dollop of whatever you fancy.

Oat cookies

MAKES 24

100g peanut butter
100g butter
150g light soft brown sugar
2 eggs
150g oats
50g plain flour
½ tsp baking powder
100g sultanas

These oat cookies are made with peanut butter, but you can substitute any nut butter and even add chocolate chips or nuts instead of sultanas.

1 Preheat the oven to 200°C/400°F/gas mark 6. Line 2 baking sheets with baking parchment.

2 Put the butter, peanut butter and sugar into a bowl together and beat really well until smooth.

3 Add the eggs and beat once more until very soft.

4 Fold in the oats, flour and baking powder and mix until it just starts to form a dough.

5 Add the sultanas and mix really well until it forms a firm dough, then take small, even spoonfuls and dollop them onto the baking sheets. You need to make sure that there is a gap of about 4cm between each cookie as they will spread as they cook.

6 Bake in the oven for 12–15 minutes until golden brown and set around the edges. Leave on the baking sheets to cool before serving the cookies.

Tips
You can substitute any nut butter for peanut butter, or if you don't want to use peanut butter, use all butter. You can add raisins, chopped apricots or dried cranberries instead of sultanas, or even chocolate chunks if you fancy it.

Freezer oaty bars

MAKES 24

225g jumbo rolled oats
50g skin-on almonds
60g mixed seeds
60g dried cranberries
50g chocolate or plain rice
    pops
100g agave nectar
100g peanut butter
125g honey

This seems a little odd, but make these and keep them in the freezer for unexpected guests, or for when you just fancy a little sweet something. Eat them straight from the freezer or leave them to thaw – either way they're a healthier alternative to a shop bought cereal bar.

1 Lightly grease a 33 x 23 x 3cm deep baking tray then line it with cling film.
2 Place the oats and almonds into a food processor and blitz for 10-20 seconds until fairly well broken down – you want chunks for texture but if they are too large they won't stick together. Pulse the mixture again until slightly powdery. Tip into a bowl then add the seeds, cranberries and cereal and stir the mixture really well.
3 Set aside, then place the agave, peanut butter and honey into a small saucepan and melt together over a medium heat. Pour this over the oat mixture then mix well with a spoon. Leave to cool slightly, then mix with your hands to make sure all the oats are coated in the peanut butter mixture.
4 Tip into the tray and spread out evenly. Lay a sheet of cling film over the top, then press down firmly to squish the mixture flat. Place in the freezer for 1 hour until set.
5 Remove the top layer of cling film, then tip out onto a board, remove the remaining cling film and cut into 24 bars.
6 To store, layer up the bars between sheets of greaseproof paper and place in a sealed box in the fridge. They can also be kept in the freezer for up to 3 months.

Tips
- If you don't have a food processor, these bars can be made with porridge oats that are already broken down and roughly chopped nuts.
- Using peanut butter instead of butter means less calories, lower fat and higher protein levels, making this recipe a healthier snack.
- Sweetness comes from honey and agave here, which are again natural alternatives to processed sugar.

Spiced bread pudding

SERVES 4–6

100g butter, plus extra for
    greasing
500g mixed dried fruit
zest and juice of 2 oranges
500g fresh breadcrumbs
1 tsp ground nutmeg
2 tsp ground allspice
500ml milk
150g dark brown sugar
2 eggs, beaten
2 tbsp demerara sugar

A great way to use up any leftover bread – an old classic recipe with a gentle spicy twist.

1 Preheat the oven to 180°C/350°F/gas mark 4. Grease and line the base of a 22cm square cake tin with baking parchment.
2 Put the mixed dried fruit, orange zest and juice into a medium bowl, mix well, then set aside for 30 minutes for the fruit to soak up all the juice.
3 After 15 minutes, put the breadcrumbs, nutmeg and allspice into a large bowl along with the milk and mix until totally combined, then set aside for 15 minutes until the bread has absorbed the milk and expanded.
4 Meanwhile, melt the butter and set it aside to cool slightly.
5 Beat the cooled melted butter, dark brown sugar and eggs into the breadcrumb mixture until well combined.
6 Fold in the soaked fruit and stir to evenly distribute. Pour the mixture into the prepared tin, smooth the top over and sprinkle with the demerara sugar.
7 Bake in the oven for 1 hour until golden brown and just set. Transfer the pudding to a wire rack in the tin to cool before turning out and cutting into squares to serve.

Tip
You can use white or brown breadcrumbs from any leftover pieces of bread

Oaty berry crumble

SERVES 4–6

450g frozen mixed berries
150g plain flour
150g butter, cut into small
    cubes
50g rolled oats
50g mixed seeds
50g dried cranberries
150g demerara sugar
natural yoghurt or custard, to
    serve

If you keep a bag of frozen fruit in the freezer, you can whip up a comforting crumble in no time at all. This one is with seeds and fruit for some added texture.

1 Preheat the oven to 180°C/350°F/gas mark 4.
2 Tip the frozen berries into a medium ovenproof dish and set aside while you make the topping.
3 Tip the flour and butter into a large bowl and rub together between your fingertips, breaking the butter down into smaller pieces so that it resembles breadcrumbs. Lift your hands up out of the mixture as you are do this, so that you are not just squishing the ingredients together.
4 When the mixture is pretty even in size, tip in the oats, mixed seeds, cranberries and sugar and mix with your hands again, rubbing it all together.
5 Sprinkle this crumble over the top of the frozen fruit, making sure you don't pack it down too much – this will give a nice light crumble texture.
6 Bake in the oven for 25 minutes, until golden brown and bubbling at the sides.
7 Leave to cool slightly before serving with some natural yoghurt or hot custard.

Tip
You can prepare the crumble as above, but put it onto a large baking tray and bake it on its own for 15 minutes. Leave to cool, then store in a sealable container for up to 5 days – it's great to serve over tinned or fresh fruit as a crunchy topping for an instant dessert.

Fruited tea loaf

MAKES 1 CAKE

1 tea bag
350g mixed dried fruit
75g margarine, plus extra
    for greasing
125g dark brown sugar
2 eggs
250g self-raising flour
¼ tsp ground mixed spice

A classic fruit cake made with tea-soaked dried fruit, it will keep for at least a week in a sealed container.

1 Put the tea bag into a medium bowl then pour on 250ml boiling water. Leave to steep for 5 minutes before removing the tea bag.
2 Tip the dried fruit into a medium bowl and mix together, then cover and set aside to cool. The longer you can leave it, the better – the fruit will absorb all the tea and makes a really moist cake.
3 Preheat the oven to 180°C/350°F/gas mark 4. Lightly grease the inside of a 1kg loaf tin with a little margarine, then line the base with a rectangle of baking parchment.
4 Put the margarine and sugar into a large bowl and beat together with a wooden spoon until softened and creamy. Add the eggs and beat until incorporated, then stir in the flour and mixed spice until just mixed.
5 Stir in the soaked fruit, making sure it goes all the way through the mixture, then spoon it all into the tin. Press down lightly as you do so, making sure it goes right into the corners at the bottom.
6 Bake in the oven for 1 hour until risen and golden brown. The cake should have just shrunk away from the sides of the tin. To check that the cake is cooked all the way through, put a skewer carefully into the centre of the cake then draw it back out again – it should be clean with no gooey cake mix stuck to it. If it isn't, put it back in the oven, bake for another 5 minutes and test again.
7 Remove the cake from the oven and leave to cool in the tin for 15 minutes. Turn out of the tin – place a plate or board over the top, then gently turn the whole thing upside down and lift the tin off, then put your hand on top of the cake and flip back up the correct way. Transfer to a plate or a wire rack, if you have one. Allow to cool totally before slicing and serving.

Peach and cherry cobbler

SERVES 4–6

50g butter, diced, plus extra
  for greasing
400g tin peaches in syrup,
  drained and syrup reserved
400g tin cherries in syrup,
  drained and syrup reserved
200g plain flour
1½ tsp baking powder
100g soft light brown sugar
1 egg, beaten
125ml buttermilk
1 tbsp demerara sugar

Tip
Serve the reserved syrup
with the cobbler.

A cobbler is simply a light scone set on top of juicy cooked fruit.
Use a couple of tins of your favourite fruit, then spoon the mixture
on top and bake. It's great served with custard.

1 Preheat the oven to 180°C/350°F/gas mark 4. Butter a medium
ovenproof baking dish.
2 Tip the peaches and cherries into the buttered baking dish and
set aside.
3 Tip the flour, baking powder and butter into a large bowl and rub
together between your fingertips, until it resembles breadcrumbs.
Lift your hands up out of the mixture as you are doing it, so that
you are not just squishing the butter but really breaking it down into
smaller pieces.
4 When the crumbs are pretty even in size, add the light brown
sugar, egg and buttermilk and stir until you have a soft and
sticky dough.
5 Dollop the soft dough on top of the peaches and cherries – just
dollop it on top as it's quite sticky and you don't want to handle it
too much.
6 Sprinkle the demerara sugar over the top then bake in the oven
for 35–40 minutes, until golden brown and bubbling around the
edges. Serve hot or cold.

Fruit juice jellies

SERVES 4–6

1 litre fruit juice – apple,
    orange, whatever takes
    your fancy
2 x 12g sachets gelatine
    powder
100g blueberries

These are perfect for a simple kids' dessert – fruit juice just set with a little gelatine – and you can use whichever juice you have to hand. Add a handful of berries as the jelly is setting and it'll be fit for a party!

1 Tip the fruit juice into a saucepan and bring to the boil.
2 When the juice is just simmering, add the gelatine powder and whisk quickly to combine. Remove from the heat and whisk until all the gelatine has dissolved.
3 Divide among 4–6 glasses, paper cups or bowls and place in the fridge for 30 minutes.
4 Remove from the fridge and scatter the blueberries over the top of the semi-set jelly – they will gradually sink down into the jelly so they are at different heights.
5 Return to the fridge to set for another 1½ hours before serving.

Popcorn

SERVES 4–6

1 tbsp vegetable oil
200g popping corn

For the toppings
100ml runny honey
2–3 tbsp icing sugar
1 tsp ground cinnamon
2 large pinches of sea salt
2 tbsp grated Parmesan
    cheese
1 tbsp very finely chopped
    chives

Popcorn is so quick to make at home and there's nothing nicer than the smell of freshly popped popcorn. Flavour only when it's all popped – it makes a sticky mess of your pan otherwise!

1 Pour the oil into a large saucepan, add the popping corn and stir to coat the corn in the oil. Cover with a lid then place onto a medium heat and cook for 2–4 minutes, shaking occasionally – you will hear the corn popping.
2 Once the popping stops, turn the heat off and leave to stand for 30 seconds, in case there are any more kernels still popping.
3 Tip out into a large bowl and let people choose their own topping – a drizzle of honey, a dusting of icing sugar and ground cinnamon mixed together, a sprinkle of salt or a pinch of Parmesan and chives mixed together.

Gluten-free orange and ginger cake

SERVES 8–10

oil or butter, for greasing
2 large oranges
225g honey
300g ground almonds
6 eggs
2 flat tsp baking powder
    (gluten-free)
2 heaped tsp ground ginger
200g crème fraîche, to serve

1 Preheat the oven to 180°C/350°F/gas mark 4. Lightly grease a 23cm springform cake tin.

2 Wash the oranges really well then place in a large saucepan and pour over enough cold water to just cover them. Place on a high heat and bring to the boil, then turn the heat down and cover and simmer for 30 minutes until the oranges are really tender. Remove from the water with a slotted spoon, set on a plate lined with kitchen paper, then leave until cool enough to handle.

3 Cut the oranges in half and discard any pips, then roughly chop them, place them in a food processor and blitz to a rough purée.

4 Add all the other ingredients, except the crème fraîche, and blitz to a smooth purée – you might need to scrape the sides of the processor a few times to make sure that everything gets processed evenly. Pour the mixture into the prepared cake tin and bake for 30–40 minutes until golden on top and just set.

5 Check the cake is cooked by inserting a clean skewer or knife into the centre of it – if it comes out clean, the cake is ready; if not, cook for a further 10 minutes and check again.

6 Remove and let the cake cool in the tin for 30 minutes before turning out onto a wire rack to cool completely. Best served cooled with a dollop of crème fraîche.

Leftover mince pie ice cream

SERVES 4–6

500ml vanilla ice cream
4 leftover mince pies, broken
   up

You can do this with whatever you fancy – leftover Christmas pudding, chocolate cake, cookies, shortbread, even a jar of dulce de leche to make your own caramel swirl. Just remember to leave the ice cream to soften before folding the additions through.

1 Remove the ice cream from the freezer and leave to soften for 15–20 minutes.
2 Tip the ice cream into a bowl and squish it slightly with a wooden spoon. Add the mince pie pieces and stir through until evenly incorporated.
3 Return the ice cream to the freezerproof container and pop it back into the freezer until it is frozen again before serving.

Meringue kisses

MAKES 20

3 egg whites
100g caster sugar
50g icing sugar
1 tsp rosewater
couple of drops of red or pink
  food colouring

For the fillings
2 tbsp double cream
50g white chocolate, broken
  into pieces
25g raspberries, finely
  chopped
40g dark chocolate (optional)
1 tbsp lemon curd and 150ml
  whipped cream (optional)

These take a little skill to pipe neatly but when you've mastered it, you'll never buy meringues again!

1 Preheat the oven to 120°C/250°F/gas mark ½. Line 2 baking trays with baking paper.

2 Take a large glass bowl that is very clean – any grease in the bowl will stop the egg whites from whisking properly. Add the egg whites and beat with an electric whisk until soft peaks form – the egg whites should just hold their shape if you pass a whisk through them.

3 Add the caster sugar, a tablespoon at a time, whisking continuously, until the mixture is thick, smooth and glossy. Sift over the icing sugar then fold in. Fold in the rosewater and food colouring, making sure you don't knock the air out of the meringue.

4 Using 2 teaspoons, place a spoonful of meringue onto a baking tray, scraping the meringue off the spoon with the second spoon. Continue with the rest of the meringue mixture, making sure to leave a gap of 4cm between each spoonful.

5 Bake in the oven for 2 hours then remove from the oven and leave to cool. They should not be browned, just lightly coloured – as they cool they will become crispy.

6 While they cool, make the fillings. Pour the cream into a small saucepan and heat until just simmering. Remove from the heat and stir in the chocolate, mixing until smooth and all the chocolate has melted. Add the raspberries then set aside to cool a little.

7 Sandwich the meringues together with a spoonful of the chocolate raspberry cream.

8 You can also use chocolate or lemon curd to stick the meringues together. For the chocolate, melt the chocolate in the microwave or in a glass bowl set over a pan of boiling water. Leave it to cool a little, then dip the flat side of each meringue into the chocolate and sandwich 2 meringues together. For lemon curd, stir the lemon curd into the whipped cream and use this to sandwich the meringues together.

Storing food

If you want to Eat Well for Less you need to cut down on food wastage, and one of the best ways of doing this is to properly store the food that you buy. Look after it well and it will last longer and won't end up looking sad, grey or wilted and make its way into the bin before you get to it. With a little care you can stretch the food from your weekly shop and cut down on those dangerously tempting quick trips to the shops, as well as save yourself from literally throwing money away…

Room-temperature foods

Some foods are best stored at room temperature to prevent them from going soggy or deteriorating too rapidly.

- **Garlic, onions and shallots, tomatoes, potatoes and winter squash**
  Store these in a cool, dry place for up to 2 weeks; if you put them in the fridge they will lose a lot of their flavour.

The Sainis

The Saini family wanted to learn how to plan healthier and more varied meals.

- **Bananas, citrus and melons**
  Once cut, store in the fridge or they will dry out. Ideally, store bananas away from other fruit because the ethylene – a natural ripening gas – they emit will cause surrounding ingredients to ripen faster.
- **Bread**
  Store at room temperature for up to 2 days wrapped in foil or in a zip locked freezer bag to minimize moisture loss. After that, store it in the freezer. You can perk up bread that's older than a day or two by popping it into a medium oven for a few minutes.
- **Dry goods (flours, etc.)**
  Dry goods can be stored for up to 6 months, but once opened they should be stored in airtight containers.
- **Nuts and seeds**
  Store in airtight containers to maintain the right level of moisture to keep them crunchy.
- **Herbs and spices**
  Heat, light, air and humidity are the enemy of these ingredients. Whole spices can be kept for up to 2 years – they last much longer than crushed or ground, which should be thrown out after 6 months. Make sure they are kept in airtight tins or spice jars.

The fridge

Some foods need to be kept in the fridge to prevent the growth of bacteria. However, before we get to the list of which foods are best stored in the fridge, there are a few key points about optimum fridge storage:

Foods for your fridge

- **Dairy products**

  Milk, cream, yoghurt and other dairy products should be kept on the upper shelves of your fridge where the temperature is most constant. Cheese should be wrapped in breathable material, such as a paper bag or greaseproof paper, and each cheese wrapped separately.

✗ Don't pack the fridge too full, it needs air to circulate to keep the temperature constant.

✗ Don't store open tins in the fridge or the flavour of the contents will be affected by the metal – decant into a bowl or sealed container.

✔ Keep the fridge at a constant temperature of 5°C or lower.

✔ Cool down leftovers as quickly as possible and store them in the fridge when cool, not hot, otherwise the hot food will warm up the food around it in the fridge, offering bacteria a lovely opportunity to grow.

✔ Wipe up any spills immediately and clean out the fridge regularly to ensure it stays hygienic.

✔ Store raw meat, poultry and fish on the lowest shelf in sealed containers to ensure that no juices drip on any other foods.

Where to store food in your fridge

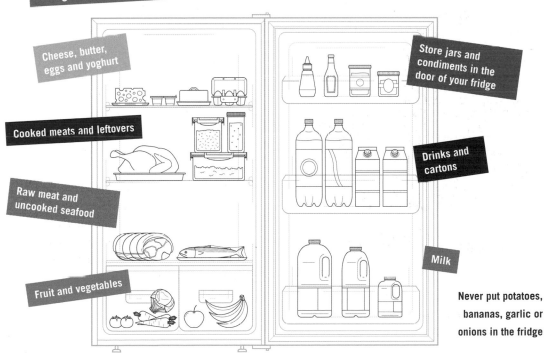

Cheese, butter, eggs and yoghurt

Cooked meats and leftovers

Raw meat and uncooked seafood

Fruit and vegetables

Store jars and condiments in the door of your fridge

Drinks and cartons

Milk

Never put potatoes, bananas, garlic or onions in the fridge

- **Eggs**

  Store eggs in their box on a shelf inside the fridge – they will last longer this way than if they are stored at room temperature. Some recipes may suggest using eggs at room temperature, in which case just take them out a bit before cooking to take the chill off them.

- **Vegetables**

  All vegetables are best stored in perforated plastic bags in your salad drawer. To make sure they don't decompose too quickly, keep them away from fruits that produce ethylene – natural ripening gas – such as apples, stone fruits, mangoes, passion fruit, pears and kiwis.

- **Fruit**

  Store in a separate drawer to the vegetables. Do not wash them until just before eating as excess water speeds up decomposition. Although whole lemons are best left out on the counter, any that have been zested should be wrapped in cling film and stored in the fridge.

- **Herbs**

  Treat basil, parsley, coriander and other leafy herbs like flowers – trim a small amount off the stem ends and pop them into a tall glass of water. Cover the tops loosely with a plastic bag and they should stay fresh for at least a week. Wrap herbs like thyme and rosemary in damp kitchen paper and layer them in plastic bags.

- **Meat and poultry**

  Keep at the bottom of the fridge – the coldest section – tightly wrapped.

- **Fish**

  Before putting fish in the fridge, dry it completely with kitchen paper and wrap it in greaseproof paper. It should keep in the coldest part of your fridge for up to 2 days, but give it a sniff before you cook it. If it smells really fishy or has an off colour, throw it out.

The freezer

The key to freezing food is to do it as soon as possible after picking or buying – this is what makes commercially produced freezer foods so nutrient-packed!

Just as with your fridge, to get the best out of your freezer there are a few key pointers:

✘ Never freeze anything that has been frozen already and defrosted.

✔ Keep the freezer at a constant temperature of – 18°C.

✔ Cool food down to room temperature as quickly as possible before you freeze it – ideally within 2 hours. Don't put hot foods in the fridge to cool down, though. Homemade food can generally be kept in the freezer for up to 3 months.

✔ Freeze food on the day of purchase and before the use-by date on the packaging. There's no point in freezing old food, it won't improve it.

✔ Pack your freezer tightly with containers as this helps the freezer to function better.

✔ Always use appropriate packaging, such as freezer bags and sealable freezerproof plastic containers, to protect your foods and prevent 'freezer burn'.

✔ Store food in portions ideally, as this means less wastage because you will only defrost what you need.

✔ Always label foods that you store – it saves eating mystery dinners later!

Foods for your freezer

- **Fruit and vegetables**

  Store freezer-ready fruit and veg in the freezer in their packaging. If you are freezing soft fruit such as raspberries or vegetables, 'open-freeze' them – freeze them on baking sheets covered in cling film, spaced apart, then transfer them to a freezerproof container once frozen. This prevents them sticking together and getting damaged. Blanch super-fresh vegetables before freezing (see box).

- **Meat**

  Freezing uncooked meat in its original packaging is the best way to keep it for long periods of time. The maximum recommended freezer storage time for beef and lamb is 6 months; for veal, pork and poultry, 4 months; and for seasoned sausage, 2 months.

- **Fish and seafood**

  Fish can last in the freezer for up to 6 months. Wrap clean, dry fish tightly in cling film, tin foil or greaseproof paper before freezing. Freeze seafood in their packaging.

- **Bread and cake**

  Slice bread before freezing and wrap in a ziplock bag or foil – you can remove slices as and when you need them. Other bread rolls, pizza bases, etc. can be stored wrapped, too. Un-cut and uniced cakes can be wrapped in cling film, then tin foil and stored in the freezer for several months. To defrost, place in the fridge overnight so that the cake can reabsorb its moisture.

- **Stock**

  Freeze stock in ice cube trays or muffin tins then tip out and store in a freezer bag so you can grab a small amount of stock whenever a recipe calls for it. You can also store leftover wine in the same way.

- **Dairy butter, margarine and cheese**

  can all be frozen, as can milk. If you are freezing liquids, allow extra space in the container for it to expand on freezing.

Foods that can't be frozen

Freezing can damage some foods because the formation of ice crystals affects the cell membranes. Although this has no adverse effects in terms of the safety of the food, the ingredient will lose its texture when it is defrosted.

Foods that don't freeze well include vegetables with a high water content, such as lettuce, cucumber and radishes, as well as mushrooms. Ingredients with higher fat contents, such as cream, and egg-based sauces tend to curdle or separate, and yoghurt, cream and low-fat soft cheese will go watery. Soft herbs such as parsley, basil and chives will blacken in the freezer, although you can pack some herbs into ice cube trays with a little water if you want to add them to recipes for flavour and don't mind how they look!

Blanching veg

If you have a surplus of veg from the allotment or market, clean and chop them then plunge them into boiling water for 1 3 minutes, then remove with a slotted spoon, drain and plunge into a bowl of iced water to stop the cooking process. This method helps them to retain their vibrant colours and flavours.

Timesaving tips

If cooking from scratch has always been offputting for you because of the amount of preparation it might take, try some of these tips to make it a little easier. Just a bit of planning can save a lot of time and effort.

It's all in the planning

Planning may seem a lot of effort, but a little bit of time spent thinking ahead will save you a lot of time further down the line.

Keep a shopping list running on the fridge or somewhere visible throughout the week and write down everything you will need to buy as you run out of it – that way you won't be rummaging through cupboards as you write your list or duplicating purchases or – worse – having to nip out on impromptu shopping trips to pick up favourite missing ingredients. That way temptation lies…. Make sure every member of the family knows where the list is, too, and get them to write down anything that they finish up so you know it needs replacing. If you find getting to the shops difficult and time-consuming, try online shopping from the comfort of your own home to be delivered at a time that's convenient for you!

Plan your meals (see page 198) throughout the week – walking into the kitchen after a long day will be much less stressful when you know precisely what you are going to cook and know that you have everything you need to hand. If you are a keen cook and like to keep a stash of recipes, perhaps order them by the time they take to cook rather than their ingredients, so you know exactly where to look when you want speedy inspiration. There are loads of recipes online or in cookery books that are designed for quick cooking.

Speed up prep time

Cooking from scratch doesn't have to mean loads of preparation and faff; there are lots of ways in which you can get dinner on the table quickly.

- **Buy bags of frozen veg**
  There's no chopping involved, you can just cook them from frozen.
- **Buy tinned beans and pulses instead of dried**
  This cuts out the step of overnight soaking and then boiling.
- **Minimise peeling**
  Give potatoes, carrots, parsnips and sweet potatoes a really good wash, and do the same for apples and any other fruit that need a wash, then they just need chopping. The skin of many types of fruit and vegetables is where the maximum amount of nutrients are contained, not to mention fibre.
- **Get the family involved**
  Give everyone a job – including the kids – and make cooking family time and an opportunity to chat and catch up. If everyone is doing something the meal can be cooked and cleared away in no time.
- **Chop once and use twice**
  If you're chopping onions and know you'll need more tomorrow, chop double and store the rest in a ziplock bag in the fridge to save time the next day.
- **Put lids on simmering pans**
  The contents will cook quicker and it will save you money on energy bills.

- **Use leftovers**
  Make them a part of your meal and that's one part you don't need to prep.

Hate the clear up?

If clearing up is one of the things you hate most about cooking, try a few timesaving tips.

- ✔ Clear up as you go – the mess won't seem so bad if it doesn't build up.
- ✔ Keep it simple – do you really need to heat your pasta sauce in a separate pan from the one you've cooked the pasta in? Do you need clean frying pans for each stage of a recipe or will a quick wipe of just one do? Ditto for knives, etc., if you don't use as many there are less to clean. (Although always be careful about using separate chopping boards and knives for raw meat, poultry and fish and other ingredients.)
- ✔ Try a one-pot recipe – these are great for chucking together loads of ingredients and will leave you with just one dish to clean!

Batch cooking

There's nothing nicer than coming home and pulling a ready-made dinner out of the freezer, either when plans go awry or as part of your weekly plan for your 'night off' cooking (see page 200).

Use your weekends or a quiet night to cook a recipe in bulk, or simply make double when you are cooking dinner anyway. Cooking ahead like this not only saves time in the long run but also saves money on energy used in cooking. Freeze the recipe in portions for another busy day – and don't forget to label the containers, otherwise your meal might be literally pot luck!

Get ahead

Batch cooking is one way to get ahead, but there are other clever ways you can save yourself time on another day. If you're cooking pizzas one day, make extra dough then roll it out and parcook several pizza bases. Freeze them in ziplock bags and you have an instant pizza base to pull out and top with whatever is in the fridge whenever you need it.

Don't forget your leftovers – so long as they haven't been previously frozen you can pop these in the freezer for another day or to add to another meal.

Parcook jacket potatoes in the microwave to save time in the oven (and cut down your energy costs, too). Cook them until softening then pop them in the oven – they will crisp up in a fraction of the time they would take if baked from raw. Think about steaming vegetables in the microwave, too, or defrosting or reheating foods from your freezer.

Meal planning

Think back to What kind of shopper are you? – did you fall into impulse buyer category? Remember, planning is at the heart of saving money, waste and time, too! Admittedly, if mealtimes in your house are – literally – a bit of pot luck, at first this sort of organisation may seem rather onerous. But stick with it, once you get into the habit it will become easier and will soon make life a whole lot simpler; doing just one shopping trip saves so much time in a busy week.

Get organised

So, where do you start? It's much simpler than you think. Make yourself a cup of tea and set yourself down at the kitchen table. Get that paper and pen out!

Begin by just planning your family dinners rather than every meal of the week; as you get more proficient you can plan for breakfasts, lunches and snacks, too, if you like. (See Breakfast, Snacks and Lunches, page 203.)

Be flexible with your planning
Don't try to nail down every dinner for a whole week, as anything can change in the daily lives of busy families – late night working, after-school activities or even having extra children on your hands. Look at the calendar and think about what each member of the family has on each night and decide if there are particular days that are really busy and on which cooking from scratch might be difficult, or at least should be kept to a simple and speedy pasta dish or stir-fry. Remember, you don't have to stick rigidly to the planner – swap the days around if you don't fancy something you intended to cook one night, but make sure you don't waste those ingredients. This is where leaving one night free for 'freezer night' works really well (see the Freezer night box on page 202).

Planning for health

The other benefits to planning are that you can control your portion sizes, which is really useful if you're trying to lose weight, and also cook filling meals that will curb those snacking urges. Thinking about what you are going to eat rather than grabbing whatever is on offer in the shop also means you can try to include all the nutrients you need to stay healthy – especially your 5 a day. If you can't work all your fruit and veg into your main course, think about incorporating them through side dishes and desserts.

Family favourites
Try to sit down as a family and make a list of everyone's favourite meals or perhaps any new recipes that were really simple and that everyone liked, and include these. Consider, too, how long each recipe takes to make and decide if you have enough time to do this – on a busy night, stick to something quick and easy. Don't forget, you don't have to come up with a completely new plan each week; rotate favourites so that they feature every week or every fortnight, to keep things simple, and make planning ahead really easy as some nights are already accounted for.

Set your budget – and stick to it

Use a note app on your phone or take a notebook with you when you go shopping and write down the various costs of ingredients, if you don't already know them, so you have a better idea when shopping of what the bill will be. This is even easier to do if you are shopping online, as you can see the cost mounting. Again, consider what's in season and which cheaper cuts/ingredients you could use to help you stick to your budget.

Make the most of just a little

If home cooking is new to you, don't go out and fill your cupboards with loads of new ingredients. Stock up as you go, and try to cook recipes that use similar ingredients – you don't want to buy an entire range of Asian condiments for one meal that will then sit abandoned in the cupboard. Equally, you don't have to rigidly stick to a recipe – don't be afraid to swap things around or substitute some ingredients that you may not have for those that you do have or even that you prefer.

Time to make those plans!

Once you've got a few recipes in front of you and you know what you are dealing with each week, it's time to fill out that planner.

Note it down

Write all the days of the week on a piece of paper and start to fill out what you want to cook. If you like, add notes about which member of the family is eating later or not at all that night so you know how many you are cooking for and when. Don't try to do more than a week at a time, but you can make a note of favourite meals for later weeks as long as you don't get bogged down in the detail for them!

Work with what you've got

Before you finalise your recipe choices, think about what ingredients you already have in the kitchen that you could use or need using up. Can you make a meal from what you've got? Check the freezer – if you get into the habit of batch cooking (see Timesaving tips, page 198) you could have a variety of meals ready made that will keep you going for a few more days, or some part-prepared ingredients.

Stretch the meals

Can you use your leftovers across the week? For instance, cook a roast at the weekend (page 136) and use the remnants in other meals. Roast chicken or turkey can find its way into a stir-fry, soup, curry, casserole or even as classic Coronation turkey (page 148). Roasted potatoes are great in frittatas, mashed potatoes can be used to top pies or make fishcakes. Maybe some ingredients will also work in other dishes, such as green beans, mushrooms, etc. so that if you are buying, say, a big bag of beans, they won't get wasted. Remember that leftovers can be used for lunch or breakfasts, too.

Keep it fresh

Not necessarily with fresh ingredients, but with a variety of different meals across the week. Try to alternate ingredients such as meat, chicken, fish or vegetables; pasta, noodle or rice dishes; soups; stews etc. over the days so that it doesn't get too samey. Eating on a budget doesn't have to be boring.

Consider use-by dates

On your planner, put meals that may need fresh ingredients earlier in the week and perhaps the freezer-based ones later in the week. That way, if you are only doing one big shop, the ingredients won't have gone off by the end of the week when you want to use them.

Daily organisation

Place your weekly menu on the fridge or somewhere in the kitchen so that everyone can see it. A quick glance in the morning means you can either whip out the dish from the freezer in the morning or any ingredients you might need later. If you have time in the mornings, perhaps you could even get ahead on some prep for the evening.

Time to go shopping!

Once you have your weekly menu sorted you can begin to create your shopping list. But before you set out, list in hand, think:

What do you have already?

Check your cupboards as you go through the recipes and see what you already have so you don't double up when buying ingredients.

What essentials do you need?

Keep a shopping list on the fridge or somewhere convenient throughout the week so you can write down things as you run out of them. That way you will know exactly what you need to buy when it comes to the time to write your weekly shopping list.

Finally, of course, take the list to the shops with you and stick to it! All that planning is a waste of time if you don't follow through on it.

If your plan goes awry one week, don't panic. Think about what went wrong and make a note of it. If you've had friends over to dinner and find yourself with lots of leftovers, think about how you can use them. If it knocks out your weekly plan by a couple of days, look at which other meals you had planned that you can swap out or perhaps even cook up the ingredients and freeze so they don't get wasted.

From Series Two, the Guest family needed to slash their shopping bills and overhaul their diet!

Freezer night

Having a freezer night pencilled onto your weekly planner gives you flexibility to switch meals and days around without hassle or, if you have stuck to your weekly plan, you can enjoy this as one night when you don't have to think about food or cooking!

So get that freezer stocked up with homemade goodies. Pick one day a week or an evening when you can cook some freezer-friendly recipes that you can then divide up into portion-sizes and pop in the freezer (see batch cooking, page 199). Remember to label each container with what is in it, the date of freezing and how many portions. If you don't have time to set aside for this, simply double up what you are cooking one day and put the extra in the freezer.

The Guests

Breakfast

It may be that your family has a very set routine for breakfast and each individual member eats the same thing every day, but if you fancy a change, have a look at breakfast recipes for something different or for a few ideas for what to eat while sitting round the table together as a family at the weekend. Add a bit more fruit to your shopping basket; it makes a great breakfast ingredient – for fruit salad, smoothies (see page 169) or to accompany pancakes or waffles. Handfuls of fruit or veg also make healthy and nutritious snacks that can help you reach your 5 a day.

Tip

If you can't give up your bacon roll for breakfast, try using bacon medallions instead of back bacon - they contain up to 50% less fat.

Snacks

Snacks can be dangerous territory; it's all too easy to nip into a shop and pick up a processed snack that's full of sugar or salt – not to mention expensive. Making your own snacks to eat in moderation is the perfect opportunity to try to meet your 5 a day and introduce healthy habits at the same time.

Again, plan ahead. Try to make a few nutritious treats that can be stored for the week or even frozen to be pulled out in the morning for the kids after school – Oat Cookies (see page 175) or Freezer Oaty Bars (see page 176) can get healthy protein and fibre into your kids' diet. A Fruited Tea Loaf (see page 181) makes a delicious snack mid-morning with a coffee for adults or for kids between meals. Get the kids involved in cooking these treats and make it a fun family activity.

Lunch

Lunches may be different things to different people – you may have to make up packed lunches for your children, or perhaps they have school lunches. Of course, it also saves you a lot of money to take lunch to work with you rather than buy it on the way or nipping out in your lunch hour. If you make your own lunch (and you really should if you want to Eat Well for Less!), you might want to plan ahead for healthy, varied lunches or just keep it simple with your favourite option. Don't forget that some dinner leftovers can work really well for lunch too the next day – think pasta for pasta salad, Couscous Salad (see page 82) or Frittata (see page 84) or mini Quiches (see page 100), which are delicious cold, too. There are soup recipes (see pages 107 and 149) that can make a great lunch at home or can be carried to work on chilly days. If you've got leftover veg from dinner one night you can easily blend it up with some stock to make a healthy soup.

Think about how desserts can provide snacks for the week, too – make extra lemon shortbread when you are making Gluten-free Lemon Shortbread with Lemon and Blueberry Fool (see page 164) or buy extra fruit. If you have too much fruit, don't worry, any left over can be blended up to make a smoothie for breakfast or any time of day, or even frozen to make a healthy ice lolly.

If you're settling down to a film with the kids at the weekend, don't buy bags of salty crisps or sugary or salty processed popcorn, make your own for a fraction of the cost. A bag of popping corn can last for a really long time and is so easy to cook and flavour to your liking (see page 186), or make Vegetable Crisps (see page 159) or Veggie Tempura (see page 160) to munch on.

Sample meal plans

To get you started, here are 2 weeks of meal planners, using recipes from this book. Desserts are provided here for each night, but feel free to leave them out if you prefer. Choose your favourite fruits for a fruit salad, and perhaps serve it up with some plain yoghurt, if you like. Don't forget that any extra fruit you buy can make great snacks or additions to perk up a boring breakfast, as well as help you to get to your 5 a day.

Freezer nights aren't listed here, but choose one of the recipes that could be frozen and prep it in advance for the freezer to give you a night off! The weeks start on a Sunday, so you can have Saturday to go shopping and cook for a freezer night over the weekend. Of course, the plan is flexible, so mix and match it to whatever works for you.

Don't forget that fruit and veg can be bought tinned or frozen as well as fresh, which will reduce wastage on a busy week when things don't go to plan.

Week 1

- **Sunday**
  Shepherd's Pie (page 35) and Zesty Peas
  (page 76)
  Gluten-Free Orange and Ginger Cake
  (page 188)

- **Monday**
  Leftover Ham Croquettes (p 156) and a green
  salad
  Gluten-free Lemon Shortbread with Lemon and
  Blueberry Fool (page 164)

- **Tuesday**
  Homemade Chicken Nuggets (page 104) and
  Oven Chips (page 46)
  Fruit salad

- **Wednesday**
  Pasta with Tomato and Basil Sauce (page 90)
  Banana and Peanut Butter Ice Cream
  (page 166)

- **Thursday**
  Chicken and Green Bean Casserole (page 37)
  Peach and Cherry Cobbler (page 183)

- **Friday**
  Thai Salmon and Bean Curry (page 74)
  Fruit Juice Jellies (page 184)

- **Saturday**
  Veggie Pizza (page 70)
  Gluten-free Orange and Ginger Cake (page
  188)

Week 1 Shopping list

Meat and fish

5 chicken thighs
4 boneless, skinless chicken breasts
500g salmon fillets
450g lean minced lamb
75g ham

Fruit and vegetables

4 onions
2 red onions
2 garlic bulbs
3 birds eye chillies
1 red chilli
1.5kg potatoes
600g sweet potatoes
1 red pepper
100g mushrooms
8 carrots
700g green beans
2 courgettes
80g frozen spinach
150g sweetcorn (frozen or tinned)
400g frozen peas
green salad
2 handfuls basil leaves
handful coriander
handful mint
handful parsley
5cm piece fresh root ginger
3 spring onions
green salad

3 lemons
2 limes
2 large oranges
Mixed favourite fruit for fruit salad – tinned or fresh/frozen
260g blueberries
4 bananas
400g tin peaches in syrup
400g tin cherries in syrup

Dairy

200g mozzarella
200g crème fraîche
75ml semi-skimmed milk
290g butter
125ml buttermilk
400g 0%-fat Greek yoghurt
a dozen eggs

Storecupboard ingredients

vegetable oil
rapeseed oil
olive oil
tomato ketchup
lamb or beef stock cubes
soy sauce
1 litre fruit juice – apple/orange etc.
ground ginger
ground cumin
ground coriander

ground cinnamon
paprika
cayenne pepper
chilli powder
3 x 400g tins chopped tomatoes
250g passata
tomato purée
500g dried pasta
400ml tin reduced-fat coconut milk
pesto
split red lentils
200g fresh breadcrumbs
2 x 12g sachets gelatin
baking powder
vanilla extract
300g plain flour
500g strong bread flour
7g fast-action dried yeast
225g gluten-free plain flour
100g rice flour
150g caster sugar
225g honey
maple syrup
almond milk
peanut butter
small bar dark chocolate
flaked almonds
ground almonds
bag soft light brown sugar
bag demerara sugar

Week 2

Start this week off with a roast and use the leftover chicken in another dinner to make preparation a little easier as well as save yourself some money. If you have lots of leftovers, use up the chicken in lunches or even freeze it for another day. Don't forget to make some stock with the chicken carcass (see page 136) and use up any veg left in the fridge from last week.

- **Sunday**
  Roast Chicken (page 136)
  Spiced Bread Pudding (page 178)

- **Monday**
  Hot Coronation Chicken (page 148)
  Eggless Beetroot and Chocolate Cake
  (page 172)

- **Tuesday**
  Smoked Salmon, Pea and Broccoli Frittata
  (page 84)
  Fruit salad

- **Wednesday**
  Lighter Carbonara (page 54)
  Eggless Beetroot and Chocolate Cake
  (page 172)

- **Thursday**
  Meat-free Chilli (page 57)
  Banana and Peanut Butter Ice Cream
  (page 166)

- **Friday**
  Cod with Warm Tomato and Olive Salsa
  (page 98)
  Fruit Juice Jellies (page 184)

- **Saturday**
  Lasagne (page 53)
  Oaty Berry Crumble (page 179)

Meat-free chilli

Week 2 Shopping list

Meat and fish

1 medium chicken
250g beef mince
250g soya mince
155g smoked diced bacon
4 x 150–175g skinless cod fillets
60g smoked salmon trimmings

Fruit and vegetables

6 onions
1 red onion
12 garlic cloves
1.5kg potatoes
500g new potatoes
200g cooked beetroot
300g frozen peas
¼ head broccoli
16 cherry tomatoes
16 black olives
6 carrots
1 celery stick
3 red peppers
1 yellow pepper
1 green pepper
1 red chilli
Little Gem lettuce
handful coriander
handful basil
handful sage
sprigs of thyme
Fruit for fruit salad – fresh/frozen/tinned

450g frozen mixed berries
100g blueberries
4 bananas
2 oranges
1 lemon
1 litre fruit juice – apple/orange

Dairy

110ml semi-skimmed milk
200g cheese
500g 0%-fat natural yoghurt
450g Greek-style yoghurt
sour cream
1.2 litres milk
340g butter
a dozen eggs

Storecupboard ingredients

lard, dripping or vegetable oil
rapeseed oil
dried basil
dried thyme
ground cinnamon
ground nutmeg
ground allspice
curry powder
tomato purée
vegetable stock
cornflour
English mustard
mango chutney

1 x 400g tin kidney beans
3 x 400g tins tomatoes
200g self-raising flour
225g plain flour
gravy granules
400g spaghetti
250g lasagne sheets
2 x 12g sachets gelatin powder
50g rolled oats
50g mixed seeds
50g dried cranberries
500g mixed dried fruit
500g fresh breadcrumbs
vanilla extract
baking powder
350g dark soft brown sugar
50g cocoa powder
6 cooked Yorkshire pudding cases
2 wholemeal pitta

From previous week's shopping

olive oil
ground cumin
paprika
small bar dark chocolate
peanut butter
flaked almonds
almond milk
demerara sugar

Food waste

In the UK we throw away a staggering 7 million tonnes of food and drink from our homes each year, which is the equivalent, on average, of £60 or six meals per family per week.

As well as not being good for our wallets, this is also a huge problem for our landfill sites and the environment, so there is now a government-backed campaign to encourage us to think about what we are buying, using and – more importantly – throwing away. According to WRAP – the Waste and Resources Action Programme – for every 3 bags of shopping we bring home we ostensibly put one in the bin. Their research has revealed that 90% of consumers are not aware of how much food they throw away – so if that's you, fear not, you are not alone!

Much of this waste is down to bad planning, but of course it's true that sometimes life gets in the way, plans change and that meal you were intending to cook just didn't get cooked. Fair enough, but rather than shove those ingredients to the back of the fridge to languish and die, why not put those top of your list of things to be eaten? If not now, perhaps they could be cooked up into something that could be frozen for later? With a little lateral thinking, you can do your bit to reduce the food waste mountain.

Here are a few tips on how to cut back on what you buy and throw away.

Before you go to the shops, think...

✔ What's in the fridge/freezer/cupboards that could be eaten up before you buy more ingredients?

✔ Have you made a list/planned the next few days of meals (see page 198)? To help you do this, as you use up ingredients, keep a list on the fridge of what you need so you're not guessing halfway round a shop and doubling up on ingredients you already have stashed away at the back of a cupboard.

At the shops...

✔ Think about what you are buying: do you need it? Do you have space to store it? Will it really get eaten this week?

✘ Don't get carried away with the offers that are on in store and come home with more than you intended to buy.

✔ Buy fruit and veg whole, not pre-washed or ready chopped – they will last a lot longer that way.

Back at home

✔ Does all the perishable food need to go into the fridge? Can some of it – particularly ingredients that are intended for later in the week – go straight into the freezer to be pulled out when needed? Remember to divide up larger packets into smaller, more easily used portions before freezing.

✔ Can you cook up any new or existing ingredients in the next day or two and freeze them so you don't waste them?

✔ Organise your fridge/cupboards so that the newly bought items are behind the existing ingredients in the fridge that are nearing their use-by dates. That way you will see first the things that need eating sooner.

✔ Make sure you store all foods properly so that they last as long as possible – see page 192 for advice on this.

Use your leftovers

✘ Don't chuck out all those bits left over from cooked meals or from packets that you opened for a recipe but that weren't all used. Think about what you can do with them.

✔ Drop stray bits of cheese into sauces or grate them over pasta, add them to omelettes, mashed potatoes or melt over jacket potatoes.

✔ Blend lonely bits of fruit into smoothies with the last spoonfuls of yoghurt. Whiz them together for an instant drink or pour them into lolly moulds and, hey presto, frozen yoghurt ice lollies!

✔ Bananas that are heading for overripe can be chopped up and frozen for smoothies or frozen in their skins for making banana bread or even to whiz up into an instant ice cream. Apples can be stewed to make apple sauce or to form the base of a crumble.

✔ Root around for odd veggies and roast them together, chuck in some tomatoes to make ratatouille, or add them to stews or make a soup out of them. If you can't eat these at once, portion them up, label them and pop them in the freezer for another day. Old soft tomatoes are perfect for making tomato sauce or to use in chilli or curries.

✔ Broccoli, carrots or celery sticks that are looking a bit sad and limp can be perked up by popping them in a glass of water in the fridge. If they are beyond that, don't discard them, add them to a veggie stock or use in a soup. Stalks of broccoli or asparagus that are chopped off are also great for this, so don't chuck them away when you are preparing your veggies.

✔ Potatoes that are sprouting can still be used; just chop off the sprouts and any other bits that don't look too palatable, then peel and use as usual.

spicy falafel with couscous and chilli yoghurt dip

✗ Don't toss the end of that baguette or loaf, whiz it round the food processor to make breadcrumbs and stick them in a ziplock bag in the freezer for use in another recipe – savoury crumble topping or perhaps chicken or fish in breadcrumbs.

✔ End of box cereal that is starting to go a bit soggy can be reborn as chocolate crispy cakes. Use up broken biscuits in cheesecakes or chocolate fridge cake, too.

✔ Pasta makes a great salad the next day or can be reheated in a pasta bake. Be careful with rice, it can be contaminated by a bacterium. Although this is killed by heat, sometimes spores can be produced that are toxic and heat-resistant. Therefore if you have leftover rice, it needs to be cooled under cold running water and stored in a sealed container as quickly as possible. Keep it in the fridge for 1 day or freeze it immediately. Always reheat rice until it is piping hot all the way through before eating.

✔ Roast dinner – this can provide the base for several more meals over the week – added to stir-fries, pasta sauces, risottos, pie bases. The carcass can also be boiled up to make your own stock.

✔ Leftover mash can be used to top shepherd's pie, fish pie or used in fishcakes or with cabbage to make bubble and squeak cakes. Boiled potatoes or roasties can be fried or added to omelettes.

Special occasions

Every now and then you're going to want to stretch the budget for a special occasion – a family lunch, barbecue or a kids' party – but that doesn't mean you have to abandon all the good habits you've got into. Normal rules apply – plan the food, think of the numbers and don't overcater.

If you do end up with a few leftovers, here are a few tips to deal with the glut!

- **Sandwiches**
  Don't chuck them away, freeze them for packed lunches. Place them in individual freezerproof sandwich bags or put them in a sealed container separated by greaseproof paper before placing in the freezer. Most fillings can be frozen, except egg, salad, jam or any soft cheese/mayonnaise-based ones. Thaw frozen sandwiches in their bags or transfer to a sealed container to defrost in the fridge.

- **Cake can also be frozen**
  It is better to freeze un-iced cake, but if it has been iced, cut into slices, lay them flat on a baking sheet, separated, and freeze them, uncovered. Once frozen solid, transfer the slices to ziplock bags or other containers and defrost as needed.

Conversion charts

Length

Imperial	Metric
⅛ inch	3mm
¼ inch	6mm
½ inch	13mm
¾ inch	19mm
1 inch	2.5cm
2 inches	5cm
3 inches	7.6cm
4 inches	10cm
5 inches	13cm
6 inches	15cm
7 inches	18cm
8 inches	20cm
9 inches	23cm
10 inches	25cm
11 inches	28cm
12 inches or 1 foot	30cm

Weight

Imperial	Metric
½ ounce	10g
¾ ounce	20g
1 ounce	28g
1½ ounces	40g
2 ounces	50g
2½ ounces	60g
3 ounces	75g
4 ounces or ¼ pound	110g
5 ounces	150g
6 ounces	175g
7 ounces	200g
8 ounces	225g
9 ounces	250g
10 ounces	275g
12 ounces or ¾ pound	350g
1 pound or 16 ounces	450g
2 pounds	900g

Volume*

Imperial	Fluid ounces	Pints	Metric
1 teaspoon			5 ml
1 tablespoon	½ fluid ounce		15ml
1/8 cup	1 fluid ounce		30ml
¼ cup	2 fluid ounces		60ml
⅓ cup			80ml
½ cup	4 fluid ounces		120ml
⅔ cup			160ml
¾ cup	6 fluid ounces		180ml
1 cup	8 fluid ounces	½ pint	240ml
1½ cups	12 fluid ounces		350ml
2 cups	16 fluid ounces	1 pint	475ml
3 cups	1½ pints		700ml
4 cups	2 pints	1 quart	950ml
4 quarts	1 gallon		3.8 litres

*Normally used for liquids only

Weights of common ingredients in grams

Ingredient	1 cup	¾ cup	⅔ cup	½ cup	⅓ cup	¼ cup	2 tbsp
Flour, plain (wheat)	120g	90g	80g	60g	40g	30g	15g
Flour, well-sifted, plain (wheat)	110g	80g	70g	55g	35g	27g	13g
Sugar, granulated	200g	150g	130g	100g	65g	50g	25g
Icing sugar	100g	75g	70g	50g	35g	25g	13g
Brown sugar, packed firmly	180g	135g	120g	90g	60g	45g	23g
Polenta	160g	120g	100g	80g	50g	40g	20g
Cornflour	120g	90g	80g	60g	40g	30g	15g
Rice, uncooked	190g	140g	125g	95g	65g	48g	24g
Macaroni, uncooked	140g	100g	90g	70g	45g	35g	17g
Couscous, uncooked	180g	135g	120g	90g	60g	45g	22g
Oats, uncooked quick	90g	65g	60g	45g	30g	22g	11g
Table salt	300g	230g	200g	150g	100g	75g	40g
Butter	240g	180g	160g	120g	80g	60g	30g
Vegetable baking fat	190g	140g	125g	95g	65g	48g	24g
Chopped fruits and vegetables	150g	110g	100g	75g	50g	40g	20g
Nuts, chopped	150g	110g	100g	75g	50g	40g	20g
Nuts, ground	120g	90g	80g	60g	40g	30g	15g
Breadcrumbs, fresh, loosely packed	60g	45g	40g	30g	20g	15g	8g
Breadcrumbs, dry	150g	110g	100g	75g	50g	40g	20g
Parmesan cheese, grated	90g	65g	60g	45g	30g	22g	11g

Oven temperatures

Gas Mark	°F	°C	°C Fan
1	275°F	140°C	120°C
2	300°F	150°C	130°C
3	325°F	170°C	140°C
4	350°F	180°C	160°C
5	375°F	190°C	170°C
6	400°F	200°C	180°C
7	425°F	220°C	200°C
8	450°F	230°C	210°C
9	475°F	240°C	220°C

Index

A

almond milk 166
alpha-carotene 31
anchovy 91
anthocyanidins 31
apple 143
    pork and apple burgers 64
apricot, dried 130
artichoke 71, 160
asparagus, courgette and roast
    chicken thighs 132–3
aubergine 121
avocado 124

B

bacon 201
    hasselback potatoes with
        bacon 134–5
    lighter carbonara 54–5
    no-pastry quiche 94–5
    white fish and bacon
    parcels 102–3
bacon lardons
    roasted tomato, basil and
        garlic pasta 99
    shredded sprouts with
        chestnuts and bacon
        144–5
baking staples 15
banana and peanut butter ice
    cream 166–7
bargain hunters 10, 13
basil 90, 99
batch cooking 16, 197
bean(s) 14, 196
    baked eggs 154–5
    bean and vegetable stew
        36
    bean and veggie fajitas 124

chorizo and bean stew 86–7
Thai salmon and bean
    curry 74–5
see also green bean; red
    kidney bean
beat (stir) 9
beef 19
    braised shin of beef with
    creamy mash 128–9
    lasagne 52–3
    speedy bolognese 38–9
beetroot and chocolate eggless
    cake 172–3
berry oaty crumble 179
'best before' dates 13
beta-carotene 31
beta-cryptoxanthin 31
blanch 9, 195
blend 9
blini canapés, smoked salmon
    and caviar 117
blueberry 184
    gluten-free lemon shortbread
    with lemon and blueberry
    fool 164–5
boil 9
bolognese
    Puy lentil bolognese with
        pasta 38–9
    speedy bolognese 38–9
bottles 15
bread 16, 192, 195
    spiced bread pudding 178
breadcrumbs 51, 58, 63, 64,
    96, 104, 144, 156, 178,
    208
breakfast 29, 201
breakfast smoothie 168–9
broccoli 207
    Asian chicken with rice and
    broccoli 62

broccoli and chilli 77, 78–9
broccoli pesto bruschetta
    114–15
smoked salmon, pea and
    broccoli frittata 84–5
bruschetta 114–15
Brussels sprout(s), shredded
    sprouts with chestnuts and
    bacon 144–5
budgeting 24–5, 27, 199
bulgur wheat 14
burgers
    homemade burgers 65–7
    pork and apple burgers 64
    tuna burgers 63
butter 195
butternut squash 130
    spicy butternut squash and
        chickpea soup 106–7

C

cabbage, make-ahead red 143
cake 208
    eggless beetroot and
        chocolate cake 172–3
    frozen 195
    gluten-free orange and
        ginger cake 188
canapés, smoked salmon and
    caviar blini 117
cancer 26, 31
caramelize 9
carbonara, lighter 54–5
carotenoids 31
carrot 36–8, 40, 43, 53, 57, 65,
    108, 128, 130, 142, 156–7,
    159, 207
carrot and cumin 76, 79
    Parmesan roast carrots and
        parsnips 140–1

roast carrots 136–7
cash and carry 18
casserole
    chicken and green bean
    casserole 37
    five-a-day Moroccan
        casserole with Swiss
        chard and couscous
        130–1
cauliflower 36
caviar and smoked salmon blini
    canapés 117
celery 38, 53, 128, 207
cheese 16, 71, 114, 193
    Cheddar 53, 60, 94, 125
    cheese twists 112–13
    frozen 195
    mozzarella 70–1, 101,
        114–15, 122
    see also Parmesan cheese
cherry and peach cobbler
    182–3
chestnuts and shredded
    sprouts with bacon 144–5
chicken 8, 19
    chicken and chickpea
        curry 105
    chicken fajitas 125
    chicken and green bean
        casserole 37
    chicken satay noodles 42–3
    homemade chicken
        nuggets 104
    hot coronation turkey 148
    leftover chicken stir-fry with
        sesame noodles 157
    make-ahead gravy 142
    roast chicken dinner with
        trimmings 136–9
    roast chicken thighs with
        asparagus and
        courgette 132–3
    spiced chicken with roasted
        vegetable rice 44–5

sticky chicken and veg
    kebabs 120–1
Tandoori chicken skewers
    68–9
chickpea 130
    chicken and chickpea
        curry 105
    chickpea crust pizza 71
    spicy butternut squash and
        chickpea soup 106–7
    spicy falafel with couscous
        and chilli yoghurt dip
        152–3
chilli
    chilli dip 160–1
    chilli yoghurt dip 152–3
chilli, meat-free 56–7
chips three ways 46–9
chocolate 166
    chocolate cookies 170–1
    Christmas meringue kisses
        190–1
    eggless beetroot and
        chocolate cake 172–3
    see also white chocolate
chorizo 71
    chorizo and bean stew
        86–7
chowder, Gregg Wallace's
    haddock 88–9
Christmas
    Christmas meringue kisses
        190–1
    Christmas seafood platter
        116–17
clearing up 9, 197
cobbler, peach and cherry
    182–3
cocoa powder 15, 172
coconut milk 15, 43, 74
cod with warm tomato and olive
    salsa 98
comfort zones, stepping outside
    of your 18

condiments 15
convenience food 11, 13, 19,
    24
convenience shoppers 11, 13
cookies
    chocolate 170–1
    oat 174–5
cooking times 8
courgette 40, 45, 60, 71, 105,
    121, 130, 159, 160
    roast chicken thighs with
        asparagus and
        courgette 132–3
couscous 14, 121
    couscous salad with
        salmon 82–3
    five-a-day Moroccan
        casserole with Swiss
        chard and couscous
        130–1
    spicy falafel with couscous
        and chilli yoghurt dip
        152–3
cranberry, dried 176, 179
creaming 9
crisps, vegetable 158–9
croquettes, leftover ham 156
cross-contamination 8
crumble, oaty berry 179
curry
    chicken and chickpea 105
    Thai salmon and bean 74–5

D

dairy products 16, 193–5
    see also specific dairy
        products
dinners 30
dips
    chilli 160–1
    chilli yoghurt 152–3
dried fruit 26, 29, 130, 178,
    181

E

egg(s) 16, 82–3, 84–5, 94–5, 188
   baked eggs 154–5
   storage 194
equipment 22–3
ethylene 194

F

fajitas
   bean and veggie 124
   chicken 125
falafel, couscous and chilli yoghurt dip 152–3
farro 14
feta 154
fibre 26
fish 8
   frozen 16, 19, 195
   Parmesan-crumbed fish 96–7
   salmon fishcakes 50–1
   storage 194
   tinned 15
   white fish and bacon parcels 102–3
   see also cod; salmon; tuna
five-a-day 26–7, 29–31, 130–1
flour 15, 192
fold in 9
food swaps 25
food waste 206–8
fool, lemon and blueberry 164–5
freezer ingredients 8, 16, 19, 26, 194–5, 197, 207
   foods that can't be frozen 195
   leftovers 208
freezer night 198, 200, 202
freezer oaty bars 176–7
fridge ingredients 8, 16, 193–4, 206–7
frittata, smoked salmon, pea and broccoli 84–5
fruit
   breakfast smoothie 169
   dried 26, 29, 130, 178, 181
   eating the rainbow 30–1
   five-a-day 26–7, 29–31
   frozen 16, 195
   leftover 207
   portion sizes 26
   seasonal 19, 28
   storage 192, 194
   tinned 15
   see also specific fruit
fruit juice 26
   fruit juice jellies 184–5
fruited tea loaf 180–1

G

garlic 192
   roasted garlic mayonnaise and lemon prawns 116
   roasted tomato, basil and garlic pasta 99
ginger and orange gluten-free cake 188
gluten-free recipes
   lemon shortbread with lemon and blueberry fool 164–5
   orange and ginger cake 188
grains 14
gravy, make-ahead 142
green bean 36, 152, 157
   chicken and green bean casserole 37
grow your own 25

H

haddock chowder, Gregg Wallace's 88–9
ham croquettes 156
healthy eating 26–8, 198
herbs 15, 25, 192, 194, 195
honey 15, 176, 188
   parsnips and honey 77, 78–9

I

ice cream
   banana and peanut butter 166–7
   leftover mince pie 189
impulse buyers 10, 12, 13
ingredients 8, 199, 200
   choice of 18–20
   food swaps 25
   types of 14–16
   wasted 206
isothiocyanates 31

J

jars 15
jellies, fruit juice 184–5
junk food 11

K

kebabs, sticky chicken and veg 120–1

L

lamb
   meatballs 58–9
   shepherd's pie 34–5
lasagne 52–3
leek 36, 88–9
leftovers 9, 25, 147–61, 197, 199–200, 207–8
   leftover chicken stir-fry with sesame noodles 157
   leftover chips 47, 48–9

leftover mince pie ice
cream 189
Sunday lunch leftovers
148–9
lemon
gluten-free lemon
shortbread with lemon
and blueberry fool
164–5
roasted garlic mayonnaise
and lemon prawns 116
lentil(s) 34–5
Puy lentil bolognese with
pasta 38–9
locally grown produce 18
lunches 30, 201
lutein 31
lycopene 31

M

margherita pizza topping 70
marinate 9
markets 18
mayonnaise, roasted garlic 116
meal planning 198–205
sample meal plans 202–5
meat 8
cuts of 19
frozen 16, 195
storage 193, 194
see also specific meat types
meat thermometers 8
meat-free chilli 56–7
meat-free eating 25
meatballs 58–9
meringue kisses, Christmas
190–1
milk 169, 178, 193
mince pie ice cream 189
mozzarella 70–1, 101, 122
mozzarella bruschetta
114–15
mushroom 71, 105, 124

N

noodles 14
chicken satay noodles 42–3
leftover chicken stir-fry with
sesame noodles 157
nuggets, homemade chicken
104
nuts 15, 192

O

oat(s) 15
freezer oaty bars 176–7
oat cookies 174–5
oaty berry crumble 179
rolled 169, 176, 179
offers 10, 12, 13, 20, 24, 206
oils 15
olive 71, 91
cod with warm tomato and
olive salsa 98
online shopping 12
orange 178
gluten free orange and
ginger cake 188
organisational skills 198–200

P

pan-fry 9
pans 22, 196
parboil 9, 197
Parmesan cheese 96, 96–7,
103, 114, 140–1
Parmesan roast carrots and
parsnips 140–1
Parmesan-crumbed fish
96–7
parsnip
Parmesan roast carrots and
parsnips 140–1
parsnips and honey 77,
78–9

passata 40, 70, 101
pasta 8, 14, 208
homemade pasta sauces
90–3
lasagne 52–3
lighter carbonara 54–5
meatballs 58–9
Puy lentil bolognese with
pasta 38–9
roasted tomato, basil and
garlic pasta 99
sausage and tomato pasta
108–9
speedy bolognese 38–9
tuna and veg pasta bake
60–1
pastry see puff pastry
pâté
smoked salmon 116
turkey 150–1
peach and cherry cobbler
182–3
peanut butter 175, 176
banana and peanut butter
ice cream 166–7
pearl barley 14
pea(s) 54, 60, 82, 88
smoked salmon, pea and
broccoli frittata 84–5
zesty peas 76, 78
peeling 196
pepper
green 57, 71
red 45, 71, 105, 121, 124,
125, 130, 136–7, 160
roast pepper 136–7
yellow 57, 130, 160
pester power 11
pesto 71, 90
broccoli pesto bruschetta
114–15
tomato and pesto pizza
topping 122
phytochemicals 31

pies
    leftover mince pie ice cream
        189
    shepherd's pie 34–5
pizza 197
    chickpea crust pizza 71
    Italian-style pizza 71
    margherita pizza 70
    pizza three ways 70–3
    puff pastry pizza bites
        122–3
    Spanish-style pizza 71
    veggie pizza 71
planning meals 7, 12, 20, 24,
    196, 198–205, 206
popcorn 186–7
pork and apple burgers 64
portion size 26, 198
potato 36, 192
    creamy mash potato 128–9
    Gregg Wallace's haddock
        chowder 88–9
    hasselback potatoes with
        bacon 134–5
    Italian-style pizza 71
    jacket potato 197
    leftover chips 47, 48–9
    leftover ham croquettes 156
    leftover potato 207, 208
    oven chips 46, 48–9
    roast potatoes 137, 139
    salmon fishcakes 51
    shepherd's pie 34–5
poultry
    cuts of 19
    frozen 16, 195
    storage 194
    see also chicken; turkey
prawn, roasted garlic
    mayonnaise and lemon
    prawns 116
prep time, speeding up 196–7
puff pastry
    cheese twists 112–13

puff pastry pizza bites
    122–3
pulses 14, 196
purée 9
puttanesca 91

Q

quiche, no-pastry 94–5
quinoa 14

R

rainbow chard 130
rainbow, eating the 30, 31
raspberry, Christmas meringue
    kisses 190–1
ready meals 19, 24
red cabbage, make-ahead 143
red kidney bean 57, 65, 124,
    152
reduce 9
reheating 9
rice 14, 105, 208
    Asian chicken with rice and
        broccoli 62
    microwave tomato risotto
        100–1
    spiced chicken with roasted
        vegetable rice 44–5
risotto, microwave tomato
    100–1
roasting 9
room-temperature foods 192
rub in 9

S

salads 25, 30
    couscous salad with salmon
        82–3
salmon
    couscous salad with salmon
        82–3

salmon fishcakes 50–1
    smoked salmon, pea and
        broccoli frittata 84–5
    smoked salmon and caviar
        blini canapés 117
    smoked salmon pâté 116
    Thai salmon and bean curry
        74–5
salsa, warm tomato and olive 98
sandwiches 208
satay noodles, chicken 42–3
sauces, homemade pasta 90–3
sausage and tomato pasta
    108–9
sauté 9
scones, leftover vegetable 149
seafood
    Christmas seafood platter
        116–17
    frozen 195
seasonal produce 19, 28
seasonings 15
seeds 15, 176, 179, 192
sesame noodles with leftover
    chicken stir-fry 157
shepherd's pie 34–5
shopper types 10–13
shopping lists 12, 24, 200, 203,
    205
shortbread, gluten-free lemon
    shortbread with lemon and
    blueberry fool 164–5
sides with a twist 76–9
simmer 9
skewers, Tandoori chicken 68–9
slow cookers 23
slow-cooking 19
smoothies 29
    breakfast smoothie 168–9
snacks 26, 27, 29, 201
soup 30
    leftover vegetable soup 149
    spicy butternut squash and
        chickpea soup 106–7

sour cream 116, 117, 122

soya mince, meat-free chilli 56–7

special occasions 208

spices 15, 192

spinach 43, 71, 82

steam 9

stew 9

   bean and vegetable 36

   chorizo and bean 86–7

stir-fries 9, 30

   leftover chicken stir-fry with sesame noodles 157

stock, frozen 195

store cupboard ingredients 14–15

storing food 9, 20, 24, 192–5

'stuck in a rut' shoppers 11, 13

sugar snap pea 43

sultana 130, 175

supermarkets 11, 12, 18

swede 149

sweet potato 37, 159

   sweet potato chips 46, 49

sweetcorn 43, 71, 82, 152, 156, 160

Swiss chard, five-a-day Moroccan casserole with Swiss chard and couscous 130–1

T

tea loaf, fruited 180–1

tempura, veggie tempura with chilli dip 160–1

throwaway shoppers 10, 13

timesaving tips 196–7

tins 14–15, 27, 196

tomato 192

   baked eggs 154–5

   bean and veggie fajitas 124

   chicken and chickpea curry 105

chickpea crust pizza 71

chorizo and bean stew 86–7

cod with warm tomato and olive salsa 98

five-a-day Moroccan casserole 130–1

lasagne 53

meat-free chilli 56–7

meatballs 58

microwave tomato risotto 100–1

puttanesca 91

Puy lentil bolognese with pasta 38–9

roasted tomato, basil and garlic pasta 99

sausage and tomato pasta 108–9

shepherd's pie 34–5

spiced chicken with roasted vegetable rice 45

sticky chicken and veg kebabs 120–1

tomato and basil sauce 70, 90

tomato bruschetta 114–15

tomato and pesto topping 122

tuna and veg pasta bake 60–1

see also passata

tortilla wraps 124, 125

tuna

   tuna burgers 63

   tuna and veg pasta bake 60–1

turkey

   chicken satay noodles 43

   hot coronation turkey 148

   turkey pâté 150–1

U

'use by' dates 13, 20, 199

V

vanilla 15

variety 199

vegetables

   blanching 195

   eating the rainbow 30–1

   five-a-day 26–7, 29–31

   fresh 16

   frozen 16, 195, 196

   leftover 207

   portion sizes 26

   seasonal 19, 28

   storage 192, 194

   tinned 14

   vegetable crisps 158–9

   see also specific vegetables

vegetarian meals 25

veggie pizza 71

veggie tempura with chilli dip 160–1

vinegars 15

W

weight loss 198

whisking 9

white chocolate, Christmas meringue kisses 190–1

woks 22

Y

yoghurt 105, 124, 148, 164, 172, 193

   chilli yoghurt dip 152–3

Yorkshire pudding 138–9, 148

The Warners

The Guests

The Scotts

The Sainis

The Austins

The Booths

The Parsons

The Stantons

The Goffs

Acknowledgements

Thank you to the wonderful, talented teams at RDF Television who make 'Eat Well For Less?' the success it is. It really is a fantastic team effort and I'm full of admiration for your incredible hard work, creativity, humour and attention to detail.

Huge thank you to Gregg Wallace and Chris Bavin for putting your faith and trust in us and being a joy to work with.

And to Tom Edwards and Lindsay Bradbury from the BBC for your unwavering encouragement. Jim Allen – boss, friend and TV guru – and Fiona Gay, who worked out how to make it all happen.

Jen Fazey (plate spinning supremo) and Janet Brinkworth (cook and comfort blanket) for all their help in pulling this book together.

Thank you to the many families who have taken part, made us endless cups of tea and handed over your receipts. I hope you're all still eating well for less.

Like a lot of working parents, I really couldn't do my job without the love, support and understanding of the home team – Matty, Rob, Mum and Dad - all of whom can cook much better than me. Thank you for keeping me sane.

Jo Scarratt-Jones

1 3 5 7 9 10 8 6 4 2

BBC Books, an imprint of Ebury Publishing
20 Vauxhall Bridge Road,
London SW1V 2SA

BBC Books is part of the Penguin Random House group of companies whose addresses can be found at global.
penguinrandomhouse.com

Penguin
Random House
UK

This book is published to accompany the television series entitled Eat Well For Less? first broadcast on BBC One in 2015

Commissioning Editor: Tom Edwards
Executive Producer: Jo Scarratt-Jones
Series producers: Fiona Gay and Jen Fazey

First published by BBC Books in 2016

www.penguin.co.uk

A CIP catalogue record for this book is available from the British Library

ISBN 9781785941658

Contributing Writer: Helena Caldon
Commissioning Editor: Albert DePetrillo
Editor: Charlotte Macdonald
Design: Gemma Wilson
Food photography: Howard Shooter
Food Stylist: Kate Blinman
Home Economist: Janet Brinkworth

Printed and bound by Firmengruppe APPL, aprinta druck, Wemding, Germany

Penguin Random House is committed to a sustainable future for our business, our readers and our planet. This book is made from
Forest Stewardship Council® certified paper.

MIX
Paper from
responsible sources
FSC® C018179